The COMPANY WE KEEP

The COMPANY WE KEEP

True Friendship and Why It Matters

MICHAEL PAKALUK

Published by Scepter Publishers, Inc.
info@scepterpublishers.org
www.scepterpublishers.org
800-322-8773
New York

Cover Image: Kamisaka Sekka, Cho senshu (One Thousand Butterflies), 1904 (detail).
Cover Design: DeLight Design Studio
Text Design and Pagination: PerfecType, Nashville, TN

Paperback ISBN: 978-1-59417-578-7
Ebook ISBN: 978-1-59417-579-4
Library of Congress Control Number: 2025936401

Printed in the United States of America

To Bill Kirk

In memory of Pfc. Richard E. Kraus, USMC.

"By his prompt action and great personal valor in the face of almost certain death, he saved the lives of his three companions, and his loyal spirit of self-sacrifice reflects the highest credit upon himself and the U.S. Naval Service. He gallantly gave his life for his comrades."

–Congressional Medal of Honor Citation for his service on Peleliu

CONTENTS

PREFACE

The point of this book is to help you, as a Christian, live better, as a friend. To do so, it helps to understand first *what friendship is*. Christian friendship is the sanctification of a prior human reality, friendship. Therefore, the "theory" of what friendship is must come before the "practice" of friendship.

But where can we get this "theory"? We will draw it mainly from the thought of Aristotle. The reason is that in classical thought, one generally finds a truer account of human social nature than in modern thought, and Aristotle is the great guide among classical philosophers.

In doing so, we follow St. Thomas Aquinas, who builds his account of love and friendship on Aristotle. We follow Pope St. John Paul II, whose view of marriage in *Love and Responsibility* is inspired by Aristotle. We follow Pope Benedict XVI, who proposed in his famous Regensburg address that by divine providence Christian revelation was meant to be "Hellenized."[1] And we follow St. John Henry Newman, who wrote:

> While the world lasts, will Aristotle's doctrine on these matters last, for he is the oracle of nature and of truth. While

1. Benedict XVI, "Meeting with the Representatives of Science," Aula Magna of the University of Regensburg (September 12, 2006). www.vatican.va.

> we are men, we cannot help, to a great extent, being Aristotelians, for the great Master does but analyze the thoughts, feelings, views, and opinions of humankind. He has told us the meaning of our own words and ideas, before we were born. In many subject-matters, to think correctly is to think like Aristotle; and we are his disciples whether we will or no, though we may not know it.[2]

Our own culture's thinking about friendship is badly impoverished. It needs to be informed by classical reflections. We tend to sentimentalize relationships, making emotions paramount rather than rational desire, that is to say, the will. We confuse love with liking; niceness with goodness; flattery with friendship. We tend to confuse goodness with what we not incorrectly call *value*. We presume, with good reason, that values are subjective. We might suppose, or might carry over from what we have been taught from Hobbes or Freud, that human beings are inherently selfish, that they will cooperate with one another only if compelled to do so by social norms which have rewards and punishments attached. We accept an untenable dualism between public and private. For instance, we cannot understand how a personal relationship like a marriage can at the same time be an institution. We have no idea what it means to say that in becoming married a couple agrees to relate in the manner of a preordained, natural institution.[3] Despite our acknowledgement of the "ecology" of other animals, we do not

---

2. John Henry Newman, Discourse 5, "Knowledge Its Own End," section 5, in *The Idea of a University* (London: Longmans, Green, 1907), p. 109.

3. "Marriage responds to the universal fear that a lonely person might call out only to find no one there," according to our esteemed Supreme Court. Obergefell v. Hodges, 576 U.S. 644 (2015).

accept that relationships and families may have a structure proposed by nature which we ignore or reject at our peril.

Moreover, our social lives themselves are impoverished. Men relate to men and women to women in highly superficial ways. Children's relationships have become coarse and are often sexualized. Our society seems increasingly frayed by the breakdown of families. Neighborhoods hardly exist. We are uprooted, moving frequently from place to place. We increasingly live our lives on screens, through the internet, each person by himself, yet with the appearance of community. We descend into various dark addictions. The most successful persons among us build big houses far from everyone else. Our popular culture celebrates individuals, self-promoters, and narcissists; it contains no celebrated examples of great friends.

This litany could go on and on. You know what I am referring to. There is a kind of illness of individualism which affects us all. Whatever the origin of this malady—certainly the Fall is the ultimate reason—it is clear that, under current conditions, to practice friendship well we need some kind of guidance that comes from outside our own culture. In this book, we look for that guidance mainly from Aristotle, as interpreted by St. Thomas, and the Gospel.

Sparrow's Nest
Bartlett, NH
February 11, 2025
Our Lady of Lourdes

PART 1

Basic Theory of Friendship

1

Two Maxims

So then, we do well to start from insights drawn from the classical world. Accordingly, I wish to set down at the start two guiding maxims. Consider these maxims as a railing that people in an abandoned dark tunnel can grab onto, giving themselves stability and helping them to find their way out.

The first is from an early Christian theologian, Dionysius, called "the Areopagite,"[1] who said that "love is a unitive and binding force."[2] St. Thomas, in his account of love and friendship, was fond of this maxim, citing it repeatedly. Let us set down, in accordance with this maxim, that when love by its "force" (Latin, *virtus*,

1. Traditionally this person was thought be the philosopher converted by St. Paul through his Areopagus address (see Acts 17). The consensus of scholars today (of which I personally am skeptical), is that this figure is an unidentified Neoplatonist who lived in Syria, writing in the late fifth and early sixth centuries. Hence, he is usually called "Pseudo-Dionysius" today.

2. In Latin, *amor est virtus unitiva et concretiva*.

vis) causes a bond to be formed among previously separate individuals, then that bond, whatever its nature and shape, may be called a *friendship*. Take this, then, to be our first guiding maxim, that friendship is some kind of bond that is the effect of love. If there are different loves, and different bonds from these loves, then there are different friendships too. Love within the family gives rise to familial bonds; love among citizens in society, to civic bonds; love as shown among Christians, to spiritual bonds; and so on.

Already in saying that "love is a unitive and binding force" leading to friendship, we enjoy an insight into friendship that is obscured by the English language. In English, the word *friendship* has nothing to do with the word *love*. The former comes from an Old English word (*freondscipe*) which means preferring someone over others—essentially, favoritism. The second comes from a different Old English word (*lufu*) which means intense affection for someone. Thus, our language reveals nothing about the connection between love and friendship. In Romance languages, however, it is different, as it is in Latin and Greek. In these languages, the word for friendship is a modification of the word for love. Consider as examples: *amour*, *amitié* (French); *amar*, *amistad* (Spanish); *amor*, *amizade* (Portuguese). From the words themselves one can see that friendship is some kind of concretizing of love.

The second guiding maxim, also beloved by St. Thomas, and before him by Cicero and Aristotle, is that a friend is an "other self." This maxim, as we shall see better as we go along, is closely related to the second precept of charity, "You shall love your neighbor as yourself." Friendship is typically a means by which we make someone a closer "neighbor" to ourselves, so that the rule that we should love our neighbor as ourselves becomes somehow heightened, strengthened, and rendered more stable, with respect to this person, by that friendship. A spouse is someone who has been made our closest neighbor by the bond of holy matrimony. A friend from childhood, although living in another city, may count as more of a "neighbor" to me than the person who lives next door because of our past association and bond. My sibling is more of a "neighbor," by nature, than a friend from school. On the other hand, it can happen that in treating another person as ourselves, we take a first step in forming a friendship: It is easy to imagine that the Good Samaritan and the man he saved became friends afterwards. In any case, we shall find that this second guiding maxim, that a friend is an "other self," is very powerful and deeply revelatory of the nature of friendship.

2

The Nature of Love

To fix ideas about friendship, let us rely upon our first guiding maxim to build up a definition of friendship by viewing friendship as a concretizing of love.

But what is love? Our strategy might appear only to push the problem back, as love can seem just as problematic to us as friendship. But here too classical philosophy comes to our aid. We should make use of the famous definition of *love* given by St. Thomas Aquinas, which he drew from Aristotle, which is that *to love is to will* or *to wish good for someone.*[1] As we shall see, this is a very flexible definition which encompasses many different phenomena, depending upon the character of someone's will and what the

---

1. *Amare est velle bonum alicui.* I shall take *"will"* and *"wish"* to mean the same thing, except *"wish"* has connotations of fleetingness and superficiality. We sometimes use *"wish"* when we mean "in favor, but not prepared to do anything about it," as in "I wish I were twenty pounds lighter," said by someone not intending to change his diet or patterns of exercise.

goods that we will for someone are like. As mentioned, love has many different types and degrees.

And yet here again, we need to go a level down and say something briefly about the will and goodness to arrive at a good working conception of love. We defined *friendship* in terms of love, and *love* in terms of the will and goods. But what is the will, and what counts as good? (Do not worry—for our purposes, this is the last level down we need to go!)

The will is a rational power of the human soul. We have two such powers: reason and the will. Reason is a power by which we think things out to get at the truth, which we then affirm, when we arrive at it, through judging it to be true. Will is a power by which we work things out to get at the good, which we then commit ourselves to by deliberately choosing to go toward it as good. The will is therefore appropriately called "rational desire." It is a directing of ourselves toward something, but precisely in cases in which the goal is conceptualized and sought, as under a certain reasoned conception.

A good example of the distinction between rational and irrational desire is the difference between how two brute animals, such as my two dogs, and how two human beings, such as my two daughters, will size things up when presented with two bowls of desirable food. When I feed my dogs, I put down two bowls side-by-side. By habit, one bowl is taken by one dog to be hers, and the other bowl is taken by the other dog to be hers. The dogs desire the food and go after it. If one is very hungry, or by mistake is fed too little, then, after eating from her own bowl, she may try to take food from the other bowl, and a fight may ensue. But each cares only about satisfying her own hunger. What the dogs don't size up, and don't care about or desire, is whether they have been given an *equal* amount of food—whether equal in size, or equal relative to their different weights. The reason is that to form the concept of equality requires the power of rationality, which the dogs lack. They have no power to conceive of equality, and therefore they can have no power to desire equality. They are bereft of the power of will.

In contrast, human beings do care about equality. If I place two bowls of a highly desirable dessert in front of my two daughters—say, two hot fudge sundaes—they will care about the sundaes, indeed, but they also will care about whether they have received *equally* desirable dishes. Each may actually care more about the equality than the ice cream. Is her sundae the same size as the other's? Does it have as much fudge sauce? Does it have an equally luscious and bright cherry? And then, if one daughter were to suspect that she was not treated equally, she would wonder whether it was done deliberately by the person who served her or out of neglect, and whether it was a sign of favoritism towards the other or some kind of lingering criticism toward herself.

We human beings care a lot about this good of equality and the network of relationships in which it is embedded. Consider simply how much anger and desire for revenge comes from believing that you have not been treated with sufficient respect by someone else, that is, with equality. But we can regard equality as an object of desire, and come to desire it, only because we have reason. Equality is necessarily an object of rational desire only.

Next, it helps to say that "to will a good to someone" is to conceive of that good as belonging to that person and then consent to it, as so conceived, together with some degree of commitment on our part to foster or protect that person's possession of that good.

Suppose, for example, that I hear that some newlywed friends of mine are now expecting a child and I react with joy. Joy is a rational emotion. It is a manifestation of the will. Unlike mere "satisfaction" or "contentment" (which, as C. S. Lewis pointed out, can come from good digestion), it has a conceptualized object that is grasped by reason. To have such joy, I must at least implicitly refer to some good that I conceive of with my reason, such as "It is good that a new immortal being has come into existence," or "It is good that the love of my friends has found a fruitful realization in a single new human being."

Suppose, as an expression of this "good will," I send them a text message to wish them well and assure them of my prayers. Then, I am willing good to them: I am consenting and committing myself to their unborn child's existence. I express my will that the mom and this child enjoy health so that the child might be safely born. I show some degree of commitment to this desired goal through my actually *doing something*. In this case, it is by texting my friends, and in saying prayers for them. My expression of goodwill also conveys, and is understood as conveying, a kind of promise to safeguard this good. Importantly, then, my wish for their good was not inert. Right from the start, it yielded the fruit of good actions.

Because an object of the will can be conceptualized, an act of the will can be articulated in sentences. We do so either in exclamatory sentences, such as "How good it is that my friends have conceived a child!", or in sentences expressed in what grammarians call the optative mood, such as "May the mom and her child enjoy good health!" In contrast, a desire that involves mere sensation, say, the pleasant feeling of good digestion, need not and cannot be conceptualized in a sentence. Of course I can make it an object of my will that I experience this pleasant feeling, as in "May I not fall ill to the stomach flu going around my family, so that I continue to enjoy good digestion after meals."[2]

2. Once I conceptualize a desire and formulate a wish about it, inevitably what I wish for has a general form.

This is enough on the topic of the will for our purposes. If you want to study it more, I recommend consulting part 1 of the *Summa Theologica* of St. Thomas Aquinas, questions 80–83.

To recapitulate, to understand what friendship is, we defined *friendship* in terms of love, and *love* in terms of wishing goods. We discussed briefly what wishing is (the will), and next we need to say something briefly about what goods are.

Although it would be highly interesting to discuss the metaphysics of goodness, for our purposes here we can think of goods for a human being as anything that we desire, or reasonably should desire, even if we do not in fact desire it. A good simply is a goal, a purpose, an object of desire. As St. Thomas Aquinas liked to say, following Aristotle, "The good is what all things desire."

If the goal is set by our nature as animals having sensation, such as how we strive to withdraw from bodily pain, then that goal or good may be deemed a *sensed* good (or *appetible* good). If the goal is set by our rational nature, such as how we wish that our transactions with others display equality, then, as we saw, that goal or good is a *rational* good. If it is something we mistakenly sense is to be pursued, such as how a parched man under the sun in a lifeboat may long to drink the salt sea water, then it may be deemed a merely *apparent* goal or good or even a *deceptive* good. If the goal is something that I, as a rational being, mistakenly think is to be pursued—such as when I mistakenly conclude that someone has done me wrong, and I seek revenge, when in truth he acted innocently or in good faith—then my being intent on gaining compensation from that man is a "false" rational good.

Again, if my goal or good is something *frivolous*, like getting my feet rubbed on the beach, then it is a *frivolous* good. If my goal or good is something *superficial*, like that *this* team beat *that* one in a game that I just happen to tune to on the television, then it is a *superficial* good. If it is something *serious* which I seek, like what I discern to be my vocation in life, then it may be deemed a *serious* good.

The point is that goods vary depending upon how the goal of my desire varies: Qualify the desire and goal in one way, and the good may be qualified accordingly.

Goals can be ordered, of course, with some subordinate to others. St. Thomas Aquinas taught, as all classical philosophers believed, that by our very nature, all of us take as a goal the complete satisfaction of all of our reasonable desires—which was called *beatitude* or *happiness*. Moreover, he thought, anything else that we have as a goal, we adopt as a goal because we take it to lead or contribute to happiness. Hence, happiness is, by the necessity of our nature, the "ultimate" good for all of us. St. Thomas also taught, as the best classical philosophers also held, that the complete satisfaction of all of our reasonable desires can be attained only through union with God. Thus, we are able to say that "union with God is our happiness," or even "God is our happiness." Both are true: The former talks about our subjective condition in becoming happy through attaining to God; the latter refers to that attainment of which makes us happy. St. Augustine expressed both of these truths at once in his famous line from *The Confessions*: "Thou has created us for Thyself, and our hearts are restless until they rest in Thee."

A consequence of what I have been saying about "good" is that we should not be fussy or restrictive in what we take to be goods. A good, again, is anything that someone in fact wants if he has a sound understanding of his own happiness or would want if he did have it. Among goods in this sense are material necessities such as food, water, and shelter; desirable bodily traits such as health, beauty, and strength; personal traits such as skill and knowledge and the virtues; but also (remember we are not being fussy) anything else that someone simply likes or has a fancy for, such as, say, eighties music or the feeling of free fall when bungee jumping. We want to be liberal in how we understand "good," because in this way we can account better for how people act in pursuing friendship. And we need not fear that we are making any mistake about the human condition, since later on, we can be as strict as we want in making distinctions between goods, say, between "true" goods and "apparent" goods, "higher" goods and "lower" goods, "useful" goods and "pleasurable" goods, "spiritual" and "worldly" goods, and so on.

3

What Friendship Is

Having been guided by our first guiding maxim, that "love is a unitive and binding force," let's compose a definition that gives the nature of friendship from our definition of love as "to will good to someone." I will propose the same definition that Aristotle gave, in which he is followed by St. Thomas. Aristotle built up his definition in stages. We will do the same.

First, Aristotle says, suppose that one person simply loves someone else and nothing more. Let us call these persons "A" and "B" for clarity. Suppose, minimalistically, that A is a secret admirer and sends anonymous gifts to B, gifts that he knows that B will like. In that case, A loves B, by our definition—because A wills goods to B[1]—but we would not want to say there was any bond

1. It should be clear that when we say, at this stage, that "A wills goods to B" we mean only that A wills things that he believes B regards as good. Things become more complex if A thinks that what B wants is actually harmful to B, or if A does not care whether they are harmful to B or not.

between them. No doubt the gift-giver, A, is bonded somehow by his affection to the person he admires, B, but B is not bonded back, and therefore there is no bond as between them. They are not *bonded together* into a unity. Therefore, no friendship exists yet.

Okay then, let us add that B loves A also. Let us suppose that B is sending A gifts too, which B knows A will like, in the manner of a secret admirer. Now each is sending gifts to the other. Each wills to the other what the other likes and what are therefore goods. Therefore, each "loves" the other by our definition of *love.* But remember that neither yet knows who the other is. Neither knows that his own secret admirer is the same person as the one he admires secretly. In this case, A may be bonded to B by A's affection, and B may be bonded to A by B's affection, and yet there is still no bond *as between them*. It looks like a coincidence of one-way bonds, not a true unity. Therefore, even in this case, no friendship exists yet.

A bond can arise as between them only if each is "discovered" by the other and they share an awareness of what is going on. Reciprocal secret admirers are rare. But you may know from your experience that, when there are two persons like this, and then the previously anonymous reciprocation is discovered, they can go in either of two directions. Perhaps one is embarrassed that he has been discovered, or maybe both are. Perhaps one or both wished to remain simply a secret admirer. If that is so, then, once the symmetry of their affection becomes known to them, they will "break it off" and stop sending gifts. Such a thing can happen if the love is romantic love. In such a case, forming a "relationship," whereby they would become "an item," might be unacceptable to one of them, or an embarrassment, or imply unwanted commitments. If that is so, then their hidden love back-and-forth, when discovered, will not lead to the forming of a bond.

However, probably more frequently, if they discover the mutuality of their love, they change how they view their previously anonymous exchange of gifts. Now, each comes to understand his own willing of goods to the other as "in exchange for" or "answering to" the other's willing of goods to him. St. Thomas refers to this back-and-forth movement of goods, where each intends his own willing of goods as "in reply to" or "complementing" that of the other, as the *communicatio* between them. Now they will have a "bond" and "a relationship." This bond appears to them as a new good, a "common good" for them, beyond the goods that they had been exchanging. We will call this bond a *friendship*, however it forms, and whatever the character of the loves that are exchanged—because, remember, by the first guiding maxim of Dionysius we are maintaining that any bond that is the effect of any love counts as a friendship. That is simply what friendship is.

4

The Application of the Definition

Aristotle's definition of *friendship*—his definition of human bonding, social unity, or whatever you wish to call it—is tremendously versatile. To show this, let's not take an exalted paradigm of friendship but rather something ordinary and humdrum. Let's consider the case of a baker and a butcher, both of whom operate shops on the same street in a city or town. Suppose the baker buys meat from the butcher by bartering bread with him.[1] By Aristotle's definition, they have a friendship. Let's see why this is so.

Here is how it works. The baker devotes his working day to baking bread. He'd like to eat more than bread for his meals and, in particular, he wants meat. Therefore, by our definition of *good*, meat is a good for him. He wants it, and he would reasonably desire

1. You may recognize that I am using an example that Adam Smith gives at the beginning of *Wealth of Nations*.

it; eating meat is a goal or good for him; it is good. Meat is certainly not the highest good, but it is a good. Note in contrast that, for him, additional bread is not a good—say, bread offered for sale by another baker down the street—because he makes plenty of bread and does not "want for" bread; he is not lacking bread.

The butcher likewise devotes his working day to preparing meats. He himself would like to eat more than meat; in particular, he'd like some bread with his meals. Therefore, again by our definition of *good*, for him bread is a good. Again, bread is not among the higher goods for him. And, again, additional meat is not a good for him, because he does not "want for" meat: He has plenty of meat; he is not looking for meat; meat is not what he wants.

Let's suppose the butcher and baker understand themselves and can foresee well enough their wants into the future. They both see that for the rest of their lives, as far as they can tell, the one will want meat and the other bread. Let us suppose that each finds the other's fare perfectly satisfactory. The baker's bread is tasty and can be gotten there at a fair price, and likewise the butcher's meat. Therefore, it's not that the baker goes into the butcher shop, or the butcher to the bakery, for a one-off trade. They are looking to form a long-term relationship, of the butcher as purveyor of meats to the baker, his customer, and the baker as a provider of bread to the butcher, his customer. They find some rate of exchange, of loaves of different shapes for pounds of meats of different grades, which they regard as fair. On this basis, each wishes goods for the other; the other wishes goods back in exchange; they are aware that they do so; and they see that their trading relationship is a new good. Therefore, by our definition they have a friendship. It is a bond between them constituted by the love that each has for the fare purveyed by the other.

A bond is a unity. Aristotle's procedure at this point, to confirm whether a pair actually have a bond, would be to inquire whether and how they are "one" in various respects. It is characteristic of Aristotle's insight that he saw that persons can actually become one in various respects. Two persons can be one "in quantity," which is called *equality*; or they can be one "in quality," which is *similarity* or *likeness*; or they can be one "in relation" to something or someone else, which is *by analogy*. Yet the highest form of unity is to be one "in substance," which is to be *the same*.[2]

We may wonder: Can two distinct substances become one in substance? The idea may look absurd at first. But aren't relatives (for example, brothers) one in what they are? What about a baby *in utero* and her mother? Or we naturally accept that husband and wife become "one flesh." And we use the phrase "other self" to mean more than "as if the same." So, this idea of being one "in substance" looks extremely interesting and needs to be investigated further. To be sure, the idea is at odds with our notions of radical individualism and autonomy.

The butcher and baker by their bond are actually one in all of the mentioned respects:

- *Equality*. They have an equality, they are one "in quantity," because neither thinks he is benefitting "at the expense of" the other. They believe their relationship is "win-win," that is, equally a benefit for each. Moreover, they regard their individual trades as equal. A portion of bread of equal worth on the market to the meat is rendered for the meat, and a portion of meat of equal worth on the market to the bread is rendered for the bread. This equality itself is desirable to them. It is a common good.

---

2. These different respects in which things or persons can be one are the first four of the famous "categories" of Aristotle.

- *Similarity*, or *likeness*. They have a similarity, they are one "in quality," in the sense that the same general descriptions apply to each in their relationship. Each is a man trying to make a living with his work, an honest tradesman, a shopkeeper on the block, a responsible citizen of the town, a fair and honest businessperson, someone skilled at what he does, a good artisan, and so on. Each understands that each of these descriptions applies to him and is expressed in their relationship (he takes "proper pride in it," as we may say). Each understands that these apply to the other. They like that they are both this way toward each other, and their being so, then, becomes a common good for them. In sum, in their relationship, they value their reputation and want the relationship to support a continued reputation like that.
- *Analogy*. They are one "in relation" too, as shown in how they reason about their exchange. Each thinks that the good he offers to the other is analogous to the good the other person offers to him: "I convey bread to him just as he conveys meat to me," and vice versa. Each might draw analogies taken from the other person's work to explain his own work to that other person, for example, the baker might bring a very fancy loaf of bread one day to sell and explain it as "like filet mignon among bread." They come to know the process by which the other makes what he does, and each views the various steps and care undertaken in his own production as analogous. That they can draw these analogies is also understood and valued by both of them, and it also becomes a common good.[3]

---

3. Everyone appreciates that tradesmen try to understand nearly everything by analogy with their own work, and this becomes a point of ridicule

- *Sameness.* Finally, they even have some kind of unity "in substance." We shall understand two persons bonded by love to be "the same" precisely to the extent that the description "other self" applies to each relative to the other. Unity "in substance" is what classical philosophers were getting at when they said that a friend is "another self." Rendered literally this phrase is actually "different same." Does each regard the other as an "other self"? Does each somehow "identify" with the other? The chief way that one person identifies with another through love is to take the other person's good as his own.

This point requires a fuller explanation. We tend to think that the love whereby another person becomes an "other self" must be sacrificial. We have in mind something like this: Suppose that there are two pieces of meat left at dinner, one tasty-looking and the other burnt, and suppose that the mother takes the burnt piece for herself, as usually happens. She does this because her child's getting the tasty-looking piece is as good for her as enjoying that piece herself, if not better. That is to say, she takes the child's good for her own. To someone looking on, weighing things simply on the basis of the distribution of the food, it looks like the distribution is lose-win for her: She gets the worse piece, and her child gets the better piece. However, from her point of view, she views the distribution as at least no loss to her and maybe as win-win. The child is an "other self" to her. She does get the better piece, because her other self gets the better piece, and she also gets the merit or hidden glory (or whatever you want

---

in novels and films. For the fish monger, everything in life is like selling fish. For the pickle merchant, everything is like the pickle business. And so on.

to call it[4]) that comes of honoring her daughter's dignity by giving up something for it.

So then, in the exchange between the baker and butcher, admittedly, neither takes the other's good to be his own the way the mother does with her child. Neither would convey something to the other out of his own product although receiving nothing in exchange. He would indeed regard such a transaction as a loss. And yet, he does take the other's good as his own, in two ways. First, in his very choice to make and to sell a certain product, he must give primary attention to what others want and need. All business is a matter of providing to another what that other person regards as good. When the baker comes into the butcher's shop to offer bread in exchange for meat, the butcher has already, in advance, accepted the baker's wants "as his own." Otherwise, why would he have dedicated himself to preparing meats for others? And vice versa.

Second, insofar as the product of each satisfies the want or need of the other, and each sees that that is so, each will typically take delight in it. For example, if the butcher, as he is walking out of the bakeshop, tears off a piece of a baguette and exclaims how delicious it is, the baker will take pleasure in the butcher's delight, just as if he were that very man, the butcher. In this respect the butcher is an "other self" to him. Similarly, if the baker comes back to the butcher the next day and tells him how much his family had enjoyed that special cut of meat at dinner the night before, the butcher will take joy in the baker's joy, just as if he were that man—even though the baker's family and their joy were no part of the business transaction. The baker is an "other self" to him in this way. That is why, by extension, so are the members of the baker's family.

4. Aristotle called it *to kalon*: nobility, intelligible beauty.

So then, we can conclude that even this market relationship between the butcher and the baker is a friendship, because it is a bond that shows equality, similarity, analogy, and even identity or sameness.[5]

Let's be clear: I have picked an idealized example here of two skilled, hardworking, stable, and honest shopkeepers, living and working on the same street, in a small village or in a genuine neighborhood. I imagined that they bartered because in bartering there is no sharp distinction between seller and buyer. Barter more quickly puts the parties to an exchange on an equal level. But my purpose has been to show that goods and love are widely diffused in human society, and therefore so are various bonds of friendship. "Love is a unitive and binding force." It is a mistake to romanticize friendship, regarding it, say, as necessarily akin to some intense sharing of revealed private life, as shown by teenagers or lovers. It is also a mistake to regard it as primarily a matter of preferences and feelings. It is even a mistake to regard it as necessarily "altruistic," or as reciprocated altruism. If friendship can be found even in shopkeepers exchanging their wares, acting out of self-love, it is potentially very pervasive.

It has not been my purpose to argue, foolishly, that all market relationships are bonds of friendship. Moreover, it is obvious that in an economy in which goods and services are often provided by corporations rather than sole proprietors, and in which we purchase things through corporations that serve as our agents ("retailers"), we will need to look inside corporations as well to find bonds and friendships. My purpose has been to illustrate that friendship is something objective and displays the parity and structure that comes from the will.

---

5. Aristotle thought it was obvious that it was a friendship (Greek, *philia*), which is an example of the greater soundness in thinking about social relationships that one finds in classical in contrast with modern thought.

5

Two Types of Friendship

There is such a thing as natural amiability in human nature. We see this when we travel: Complete strangers smile at you and want to help. It is seen, too, in how we look for common topics for light talk when we are with random others during the day—usually we talk about the weather or some important looming sports match.

Because of this natural amiability, our butcher and shopkeeper will chat and, over the weeks and months, they will come to learn something about each other. Suppose, for instance, that they discover that they each love chess and that each has a fairly good understanding of the game. They might therefore arrange things so that, for instance, they do their business just before lunch hour, so that during their lunch break each day they play a chess match. This daily chess match could become so important to them that, supposing one of them had to change lines of work or close down his business, they would continue to meet in other circumstances to play chess each day.

Clearly, a new and distinct bond would have arisen between them, a second friendship. It would be different in kind, Aristotle says, because the goods they love are different in kind. The first bond between the butcher and baker was the result of the love of each for the good for himself that the other provided. Love of meat (of the baker) and love of bread (of the butcher) were the glue for their friendship. Aristotle counts meat and bread as "useful" goods, because they satisfy needs, and therefore he would say that this bond between the butcher and baker counts as a "friendship for usefulness," or more precisely that these men are bonded together ultimately on the basis of useful goods. But the second bond between them was the result of the love of each for the enjoyment of the game of chess. We shouldn't trivialize this enjoyment; chess is an important human good. We shouldn't think of their enjoyment, because it is enjoyment, as necessarily on a par with some kind of pleasurable feeling, like the pleasure of being immersed in a warm bath. Obviously, the pleasure of chess comes from the engagement of one's cleverness, experience, and character. Still, as we say, in the end chess is "only a game." People play it because they have fun playing it, and if they did not enjoy it, they would stop.[1] And no value to others comes from playing it.

This second bond is distinct in kind because the love which binds the two together in that case is a love for the enjoyment of playing chess. Aristotle would count the enjoyment of playing chess as a "pleasant" good. Therefore, one might say, chess-playing

1. Children who are "forced" by their parents to study chess and compete in matches, or professionals who feel "forced" to continue playing to pay the bills, after they have stopped enjoying the game, are in a different class.

friends, or the butcher and baker, insofar as they are bonded together by their regular chess matches, have a "friendship for pleasure." Or, more precisely, these men are bonded together ultimately on the basis of the goods of pleasure and enjoyment.

Two chess-playing friends, bonded together by love of chess, show the same marks of unity as did the butcher and baker:

- *Equality*. They need to be roughly equal in skill for each to enjoy playing against the other, or, if they are not, they equalize themselves, by some handicap imposed on the better player (for example, a piece is taken away, or less time is allotted on a clock). Furthermore, they are aware that they are equal or equalized and want to foster it. Therefore, their equality becomes a common good for them.
- *Similarity*. They are obviously similar, because they both like chess, study chess, and like to talk about chess. If one started to lag in his attention to the game, the other might try to spur him on, because they both recognize that their similarity in liking the game is a common good for them.
- *Analogy*. They latch onto analogies and complementarities that they regard as binding them together, such as, "You take care in preserving pawn structure, whereas I favor developing quickly." These complementarities as recognized between them become yet another common good.
- *Sameness*. Finally, each is constantly regarding the other as an "other self," insofar as he thinks that in competing hard he makes the game better for the other, and insofar as he is constantly trying to see things from the other's point of view during a match. The iteration is important here, just

> as it is in many other games and in competitions.[2] Each knows the other is aware that he is aware of what the other is doing, and so on. What we call a "feint" or "misdirection" is when one of them exploits these layers of shared understanding to do something unexpected. That their matches have this kind of intense unity of activity, and multiple levels of the containment of the understanding of the one within that of the other, is also a common good of their relationship. They are aware that it is and probably prize it above all the other common goods of their bond.

In the classical conception of friendship, there is nothing ethically suspect about useful or pleasant goods or our love for useful goods or pleasant goods. In the classical world, these loves were not depreciated as being "egoistic."[3] As living rational animals, we have needs, and we seek enjoyment. Consider as an analogy sleep versus waking: To do good, we need to sleep well, just as we need to be awake. Neither sleep nor love of sleep are ethically suspect. My wish to get sleep is not inherently "egoistic." Love of sleep simply needs to keep to its proper place and be duly proportioned. Likewise, there is nothing ethically suspect about those bonds that result from love of useful goods or love of pleasant goods. In fact, if the useful goods are genuinely useful and don't harm others, and the pleasant goods are genuine pleasures and centered around innocent activities, then, because of human amiability, these bonds can serve as conduits, along which deeper affections can flow. Moreover, humble bonds among participants in the market and among

---

2. Hence, "game theory."

3. "Egoism" was not set in opposition to "altruism" before the early nineteenth century positivist, Auguste Comte.

those who enjoy playing sports and games or other pleasures, such as fishing or music, contribute to the peace and unity of society.

Rather, from a classical point of view, the main shortcoming in these sorts of bonds is that the friends who are bonded together by them are bonded together by something other than a love precisely *for* the other. The butcher loves the *bread* of the baker. The baker loves the *meat* of the butcher. The bread is exquisite; the meat is first-rate. But the butcher does not love the baker except as a bread supplier, and the baker does not love the butcher except as a meat provider. What they each love is something outside of and beside themselves, certain "external goods" which they produce and then exchange. Their loves for bread and meat, as we saw, do indeed bind them together. That they have some sort of a genuine bond should not be denied. Bonds among us are good. And yet it is not a love of each precisely for the other that binds them. Similarly, when they get together to play chess, they love the enjoyment of chess games and the interest of their matches. This pleasurable good which they realize when they are together is something that each contributes to and plays a part in. But what they love is located in the moves of the game on the board. They produce the moves and the games they play. The game is their shared product. To be sure, their love for intense games of chess does truly bind them together. Their shared love of chess does lead to a genuine bond of friendship. But they are not bound together by a love of each precisely for the other.

It follows from what has just been said that such bonds have a certain independence from the morality, religious commitments, and political allegiances of the friends who are bonded, because these things are bound up with who we are and make us more or less loveable, for who we are, to others. This fact has long been recognized as a two-edged sword. On the one hand, it makes bonds based on usefulness or pleasure more attainable in pluralistic conditions. The trading relationship of the butcher and baker can in principle flourish regardless of whether one of them is having an affair, the one is an atheist and the other a Muslim, or the one is pro-life and the other supports so-called abortion rights. (We must say "in principle" because often disparities in deep matters do break through and put a strain on such bonds.) The economist Hayek favored economic relationships for this reason: No religious or ideological consensus is necessary to attain them. International policy is sometimes based on this consideration as well, such as the hope that trade between nations will on its own foster friendship and peace.

On the other hand, such bonds inherently lack stability. They can break up just as quickly as they can form. If what counts as useful or pleasant changes, even to just one of the friends, then these bonds dissolve. Business relationships can lose their rationale very quickly if business conditions change. People go through phases and will love chess intensely for only a few years but then lose interest. If what you are looking for is inherent stability, you will not find it in these types of relationships. If an entire society were bonded together solely by relationships like this, then its citizens would continue to feel unmoored.

6

A Third Type of Friendship

What would it mean, to love precisely this other person and not some good or pleasure he makes or produces? It would be to love him because he himself is good. But what would this mean, that someone himself is good and a worthy object of love? In the classical world, it meant two things. It meant, first, that he was naturally endowed with goods of body and soul, say, that he had a naturally cheerful temperament and an appealing youthfulness. Second, it meant that he had good traits of mind and character, the *virtues*, which admittedly may have some element of natural endowment, but which mainly are acquired through good upbringing, education, experience, and self-discipline. The virtues would include not simply the so-called "cardinal virtues" of courage, moderation, justice, and prudence, but also "intellectual virtues," such as knowledge, savvy in practical matters, facility in formal disciplines, and wisdom.

But Christians have various other grounds, richer grounds, which were not recognized by the classical philosophers. These will be familiar to you, but let us review three of them. We believe that each person is made in the image of God and therefore he or she is good as reflecting God. We believe that Christ died for each person. To be "someone for whom Christ died" is very much to be a worthy object of love. We believe that baptism confers a supernatural life and makes someone a son or daughter of God. This "divine filiation," implying a family relationship in Christ, establishes an even stronger basis for loving someone.

As Christians, we care as much about the virtues as the ancients did. But we place equal emphasis on keeping God's law and knowing God's truth. Furthermore, because we have greater clarity about sin, we believe sin can be overcome by penance and grace: "Where sin increased, grace abounded all the more," (Rom 5:20). Hence, we believe that to live one's life in the manner of a penitent ("I am an unworthy servant") also renders someone lovable and good. In Christ, sorrow for sin is just as lovable as the virtue that the sin was against. A life of penitence for past adultery is as good, and as good a reason for loving someone, as unwavering fidelity, if not better, because of the potentially greater humility and the greater love that comes from having been forgiven more. Jesus taught that tax collectors and prostitutes were entering the kingdom of heaven ahead of the Pharisees, who incidentally were widely admired in their society for their virtue (Mt 21:31).

But right now, we need not be too precise about what makes someone good and therefore potentially loved precisely for being himself good. The important point, for the moment, is that we wish to draw a distinction between two ways in which love works as a unitive and binding force, two kinds of bonds and friendships. On the one hand, there is love that binds two persons together where the love of each is for some good that the other produces, which is either a useful good or an enjoyable good. On the other hand, there is love that binds two persons together where the love of each is for some good in the other person. The latter kind of bond Aristotle called "the friendship of those who are alike in virtue." He also called it (as I shall explain in a moment) "perfect" or "complete" friendship.

Thus, there are three kinds of friendship, according to Aristotle: two where the bonds are the effect of loves for goods external to the friends, which the friends produce, exchange, and share, and one where the bond is the effect of loves for the goods that are those friends themselves.

It helps to understand Aristotle's labels correctly. In saying that there is a kind of bond between us which is of those "alike in virtue," he does not mean that the friends are similar in what virtues they have, but rather that they are alike in both having virtues. These virtues could be complementary, say, if one friend has great courage, shown in battle, and the other great prudence, shown in administration. Or if one friend is a musician and the other is a scientist. Understand a *virtue* very liberally to be simply any trait that contributes in some way to a person's himself being good, and therefore to his being in some way admirable and in some respect potentially loved by another. Again, for this friendship, the important thing is that the love that makes the bond is love for something in the other person, not for some good apart from him that he produces or that you produce together.

Aristotle's other label, "perfect" or "complete" friendship (the Greek term is *teleia philia*), is extremely interesting. Aristotle and other ancient philosophers used to say that there were three distinct kinds of things we could love: beauty, utility, and enjoyment. They thought of these as forming a sequence. Beauty gave rise to utility and enjoyment, but not the other way around. What was beautiful would be, as a rule, useful and pleasant. (We say, similarly, "Function follows form.") What was useful, too, would be pleasant: We take pleasure at least in the usefulness of a useful thing (that tool that works exactly as it should, those fresh eggs that scramble up so fluffily). But a merely useful thing need not be beautiful, and what is pleasant need not be either useful or beautiful. Thus, the instinct of classical Greek culture—and one can see it in their literature and buildings—was that, as general rule, one should aim at beauty, and then the other two would follow. It would often be foolish to aim at the others only, since one would not get beauty and would likely lose the others as well.[1]

In these remarks, understand *beauty* (*kalon* in Greek) very broadly to mean whatever is of itself worth looking at and pondering. Excellent design, appropriate relationships, due proportion and order, and fittingness—these all count as *kalon*. A valid mathematical proof is *kalon*. The golden proportion in a building is *kalon*. An organization's acting in accordance with its founding mission, fittingly so, would be *kalon*. The virtues that serve to perfect someone in body or soul are *kalon*.

Aristotle taught that the virtues show a similar sequence. Virtues by their very nature lead to plentiful good for others and an abundance of enjoyment for others. Thus, if one person loved another for his virtue, and that love was reciprocated, and that reciprocation was recognized so that a bond formed between them as a result of their loves, then the bond would also involve, as a consequence, the production and exchange of useful goods and pleasant goods. It would be as if two additional bonds were contained within that one bond. The bond would imply lots of advantages to the friends, akin to the butcher and baker, and lots of pleasures, akin to the chess

---

1. See the perceptive essay by C. S. Lewis on a similar theme, "First and Second Things," *God in the Dock* (Eerdmans, 1970), pp. 278–282.

enthusiasts. It would be "complete" in the sense that every basis for love and every kind of love was included in that original, foundational love. And utility and pleasure would be found there, but in a fuller and more satisfying realization, because these would be grounded in the goodness, the "virtue," of the persons themselves.

There are countless examples and applications of this outlook. Take for example how a man and woman when they are "dating" will take care to "do" things like go to concerts or go out to dinner. They won't get together except to "do" things—miniature golf, see a movie, hike a mountain. These are enjoyable activities external to themselves. If they are savvy, they understand that they are doing these things in order to spend time with the other, to discover whether the other person is marriageable. Whether each enjoys simply "the company of the other" is crucial for marriage. Marriage can be viewed as a man and woman binding themselves by a commitment so that all of the goods of a perfect friendship are available to each, from each, until one of them dies. Once they are married, they will occasionally "do" things. But they will have no more need of "doing" things because daily life will be more pleasant for them than dating was before they got married. Likewise, the meals that they make for each other will be a lot more enjoyable than when they went out to eat all the time. The food may not necessarily be as enjoyable from the standpoint of technical cooking skill, but it will be because of the love with which it is prepared. From an Aristotelian point of view, in such a shift—from dating to being married—the couple's bond shifted from being initially based on love for enjoyment to being based on love for the good that each sees in the other, which gives rise to a "perfect" or "complete" bond.[2]

---

2. It should be obvious that any exchange of sexual pleasures will subvert their discernment and their perception of what they love the other for.

What do friends who share a "perfect" bond of friendship exchange back and forth? Aristotle says some deep things about it, whereas Christianity says even deeper things. For now, I will recount what Aristotle says. He says, first of all, that they mainly give their time to each other. They "spend time together," "spend their days" together, and want to "live life with each other"—as Aristotle puts it in various ways, striving to express this unique action—because that is how each possesses the good that the other person is. Living life with another is essentially a contemplative activity. It is a matter of appreciating something together, more than doing something—the way a mother and father exchange exclamations about how their child looks or the way, when they are old, they may sit on rocking chairs on the porch reflecting with gratitude on their shared life. Second, he says that they exchange gifts, but they measure the worth of a gift not primarily by its usefulness to the recipient but mainly by the discernment and sacrifice that was shown by the gift-giver. The famous short story *Gift of the Magi*, by O. Henry, displays well what Aristotle has in mind. The wife cuts off and sells her cherished hair to buy a watch chain for her dear husband's special watch; the husband sells his cherished watch to buy a lovely comb for his dear wife's beautiful hair. Each gift turns out to be useless to the recipient. Yet the gifts are very precious, because they testify to the strength of the love of the gift-giver, because of the sacrifice needed to give them. What each gave up was identified with the giver. Therefore, each gift stands for that giver, himself or herself, given in those gifts.

But different virtues lead to different kinds of exchange. Some do seem to have more obvious practical upshots than others. Take courage, for example. Suppose you are not particularly courageous, and that is why you are attracted to and want to spend time with one of your classmates whom you see is very bold. He sees that you are thoughtful and have a lot of knowledge of theology and wants to spend time with you, to learn from you. You are "alike in virtue," that is, alike in each having something good in you that another can love. You find your friend's courage an object of fascination. You *enjoy* how it manifests itself in his speech, demeanor, and self-confidence. He has "swagger." That is, he provides "enjoyable goods" for you. But you also *profit* from his company. For example, he invites you to do things together, like rock climbing or deep-sea diving, that you would never have undertaken otherwise. He is "useful" to you, that is, the things he "produces"—occasions to rock climb and deep-sea dive—are things you want. But then, also, through his leadership and example, you find yourself becoming bolder. You recognize this and want to spend time with him for this reason above all. You want to become as bold as he is, so that you can answer to his boldness with your own boldness.

The example can be filled out or tweaked as you like, to make it more realistic. You can see how such a relationship is "perfect" in Aristotle's sense, and how utility and pleasure have a fuller form in such a relationship than when they are sought for and found in isolation.

Recall that Aristotle regards a bond as a unity, and he thinks of unity as oneness which is shown differently across the different very general types of being that he called *categories*. To be one in the category of substance is to be the same; one in the category of quality is likeness; one in the category of quantity is equality; and one in the category of relation is analogy. How are these types of unity displayed in a "perfect" friendship?

- *Equality*. They are equal or aim to be equal in how much they would be willing to sacrifice for the other. In the best relationships, each would give up his life for the other.

- *Similarity.* They are alike in virtue, as already said. But they are also alike in intention: If their virtues are complementary, then each will want to become and be like the other, insofar as is appropriate. A tough man will want to imitate his wife's sensitivity in a manner appropriate to him, and the woman her husband's toughness in a manner appropriate to her.

- *Analogy.* They are analogous, for instance, insofar as each understands the other through what is most familiar to himself or herself. Take skill to be revelatory about virtue in general: If an elite pro athlete becomes friends with a highly successful tech entrepreneur, the athlete sees the entrepreneur as "elite" in that domain, and the entrepreneur sees the athlete as a successful risk taker in his athletic domain. They size up not their products but themselves in analogous ways.

- *Sameness.* As we have seen, in any friendship, each friend is in some way an other self to his friend. We can think of two persons being "other selves" when each, in some kind of habitual or steady way, becomes related to the other as he was antecedently related to himself. Suppose, for instance, that I love making lattes for myself. I am truly adept at this. I make great espresso pours and great foamed milk. I do this for myself for several years. I get so good at it that I take pleasure in making lattes for friends and family. I'm known as the "barista" among them. "You should do this for a living," they say. Suppose, then, that at their urging I open an espresso shop. In that case, I have taken a service that I originally provided for myself and turned it outward toward others generally, making great lattes for them, just as I had done for myself. And many businesses have begun in this way. As the proprietor of an

> espresso drinks business, then, I am treating my customers as "other selves." I am not doing so in a particularly exalted way. I am only making them lattes, after all. Nonetheless, the customers, in a limited way, are "the same" as myself, because I make coffee for them the way that I've long wanted to make it for myself. Another limitation is that there is no longstanding relationship between an espresso shop and its chance customers. The customers become other selves only during the transaction.
>
> But in a perfect friendship, the friends are other selves without limitation. What this means is that, in a standing relationship, each assesses goods and evils for the other relative to the other's genuine happiness, as he had antecedently been doing for himself. A Christian would say that each evaluates everything in the other relative to God's law, the virtues, the life of discipleship to Christ, the universal vocation to holiness, and eternal life with God. It's not simply a well-made latte that one wants for a friend like this, but holiness and eternal life in heaven. To treat the other as ourselves is to love him "for the sake of God," just as we love ourselves "for the sake of God." The relationship therefore has no limitations in time. It is not limited to a transaction, or certain types of transactions, or certain circumstances, but persists always.

Aristotle said that perfect friendships are rare because virtue is rare. Scholars debate his claim; I am doubtful that by "rare" he was making a statistical claim about frequency. His meaning, in my view, is better expressed by saying that friendships like this form from a discerning attitude. It's like our attitude when we are serious about getting better at something. If a man is beginning to do serious athletic training and wants to learn about good form, good diet, and other habits, he won't just walk up to anyone and think he will learn the right things. He must be discerning. When parents are looking for a good teacher for their talented daughter, they have to be discerning. It would be foolish to go to listings in the classified section or on the internet looking for piano teachers and pick one out randomly, or even on the basis of a rating. Something similar holds for how they arrange for their children to make friends. They believe, sensibly, that they should try to arrange things so that their children form good friendships. They are prepared to block a child's friendship if they think it's not good or a waste of time. For practical purposes, they are regarding good friends for their child as "rare." Aristotle's point is that we need to take the same approach to our own friends.

Perfect friendships also take a long time to form, because it takes time to see the virtue in another and gain confidence in its solidity. But once these bonds form, as Aristotle observes, they tend to be highly stable over time. One reason is that any virtue or excellence that really is in another tends to be stable. Another is that, as we saw, perfect friendships contain everything within them that one looks for in bonds with others. Another is that they tend to be self-reinforcing, because of a virtuous cycle: Good friends assist each other in improving, but as they improve, they improve in improving each other, so that they become better, and so on.

Yet another, Aristotle says, is that friends in a perfect friendship are resistant to slander. This might seem a curious thing for Aristotle to fasten on. But, again, like Dionysius, he is interested in how separate individuals join together to form unities, and a unity is stronger if it can repel hostile forces of disunity. In ordinary life, a common hostile agent from without would be the insinuations and accusations of another, intended to break the friends apart by undermining their mutual trust.

7

The Moral of the Butcher and the Baker

In reviewing what Aristotle and St. Thomas taught about social bonds, I have aimed to bust through certain dualisms, those not consistent with Christian philosophy, that continue to bedevil us. These dualisms derive from unsound systems of modern philosophy. One such dualism, which derives from Cartesianism, is between "egoism" and "altruism." Descartes conceived of us as if trapped in our own consciousness. Within Cartesianism, just as it is problematic to know the "external world," so it is even more problematic to acknowledge others and deal with them as if they are real and equally real as we are. We seem caught between only two options: to be selfishly turned on ourselves or to be turned out equally to all others generally, in disregard of ourselves, viewing ourselves at best "one among many equal others."[1]

1. Thomas Nagel seems captured by this Cartesian problematic in his book, *The Possibility of Altruism* (Princeton University Press, 1970).

If we accept a dualism like this, then we are likely to hold that the only ethical relationship we can have toward others is "altruism," whereas egoism looks selfish and greedy. And then, when we look upon those human relationships that by God's design are meant to bind society together in an ordinary way, since these are not "altruistic," we may come to view them, wrongly, as selfish and disreputable. It might seem to follow, too, for a Christian, that these relationships could not be sanctified, since nothing disreputable can be sanctified. Or we might rebel against this dualism in the wrong way by saying that "egoism" must be good after all. The objectivism of Ayn Rand is appealing to many for this reason.

Another modern dualism we need to bust through is that between feeling and reason. This dualism derives from unsound systems of modern philosophy that held that ethics is a matter of cultivating the proper "sentiments." For someone attracted to this way of looking at things, feelings seem to be flexible, open, tolerant, and sensitive, whereas reason can look harsh, rigid, and uncompromising. The doctrine of Aristotle and St. Thomas on friendship busts through this dualism by drawing attention to the will, the "rational appetite," and emphasizing that the will, not feelings, must ultimately be responsible for stable bonds among us over time.

Another related dualism is between private and public. Feelings need to be private; therefore, if friendships are a matter of feelings, they must be private affairs. A friendship could not be a bond that unifies society in a public way. A bond like marriage, on this view, could not be an "institution," as it is. Generally, in the classical understanding, friendships are bridges between public and private. Or if to be ethical requires that we break out of the isolation of our own consciousness, in order to become "altruistic" toward others—and consciousness is private—then altruism will look like it has to be structural and procedural, like a system of regulations and laws. From this point of view, we lose sight of the true sources of vitality and peace in a society, which spring from families and close personal relationships.

Finally, consider the famous passage in *Wealth of Nations* (book 1, chapter 2) by Adam Smith:

> . . . Man has almost constant occasion for the help of his brethren, and it is in vain for him to expect it from their benevolence only. He will be more likely to prevail if he can interest their self-love in his favour, and show them that it is for their own advantage to do for him what he requires of them. Whoever offers to another a bargain of any kind, proposes to do this. Give me that which I want, and you shall have this which you want, is the meaning of every such offer; and it is in this manner that we obtain from one another the far greater part of those good offices which we stand in need of. It is not from the benevolence of the butcher, the brewer, or the baker that we expect our dinner, but from their regard to their own interest. We address ourselves, not to their humanity but to their self-love, and never talk to them of our own necessities but of their advantages.[2]

It is difficult to know if Adam Smith himself was implicitly accepting here something like a dualism between egoism and altruism. Regardless, we tend to interpret this passage as evincing such a dualism. We understand what Smith calls "benevolence" here as altruistic. Benevolence presumably is shown in conferring a good on another at a loss to oneself. On the other hand, "self-love" is identified with "a regard to one's own interest." Self-love presumably would be shown in seeking a gain for oneself at loss to another,

---

2. Dutton: 1910, p. 13.

or regardless of any loss to another. Then it would be selfish and greedy. This passage, so interpreted, says something shocking and deflationary: "Society is held together not by any kind of humane concern for others but by a narrow concern to advance oneself even at the expense of others." It would be advocating a version of "private vices, public benefits."[3]

As we have seen, the classical analysis of bonds of trading in the market is very different. In the classical view, every type of wishing of goods toward another, even that which is a manifestation of self-love, tends toward reciprocation.[4] Love is a unitive and binding force. Its teleology is to form a bond. Certainly, what we call *altruism* also looks for reciprocation, either from the recipient in gratitude, or from God in the form of grace and future reward ("And your father who sees in secret will reward you," Mt 6:4). Also, Smith would be wrong to identify self-love (if he does) with the mere seeking of one's own material interests. First of all, each person's "self" love extends to subjects besides himself. The butcher works to support his family, not simply himself, and the baker does so as well. Moreover, the goods "self-love" looks for extend to everything relevant to one's genuine happiness, and therefore, by implication, to eternal salvation. (Remember the famous line from St. Augustine.) Self-love must attend to material interests, indeed, it must be concerned with material prosperity, because we are embodied intelligences, but it must be concerned with much more than this, because our nature and destiny transcend this world.

---

3. Bernard de Mandeville, *The Fable of the Bees: Or, Private Vices, Public Benefits* (London: Roberts, 1714).

4. Even when we hate someone, we expect this person to hate us in return.

8

New Realities

Every human being we look at is rightly seen as a superposition of four realities, and therefore so also is every relationship among human beings:

- The first is what that relationship was meant to be in God's creation: for marriage, for example, how it was meant to be "from the beginning" (Mt 19:8).
- The second is how that relationship is marred, disfigured, and thrown toward disorder as the result of sin, especially original sin, but also our actual sins. As regards marriage, because of "hardness of heart," Moses tolerated divorce. Now, husband and wife harm each other in many ways, sometimes grievously.
- The third is that relationship considered as composed of persons for whom Christ died. Christ came to save: He

looks upon us with pity and has paid a price to redeem us. As regards marriage, this would be husband and wife as penitents, on their knees, asking each other for forgiveness, and going to the sacrament of confession for graces.

- The fourth is a relationship as lived out by Christians who are reconfigured in Christ. In baptism, we are given a divine life and can draw upon many graces for help. As regards marriage, this would be the natural institution raised to the level of a sacrament.

In the old books, the first reality was called "the order of nature." The last two were referred to as "the order of grace." And that murky middle area of contest, strife, and the loss and gain of souls was not given its own name but has sometimes been referred to as creation "subject to sin."

We have been looking at Aristotle's classical account as a window into the "order of nature." Aristotle has helped us look at social bonds objectively and freed from certain modern dualisms.

The ancients, in general, really did pay more attention to human nature than we, because a thing is noticed well when it is noticed in its place. In particular, they easily conceived of the human race as situated between gods and brute animals. They liked to wonder about what made us distinctive as occupying that middle position. When pilgrims in pagan Greece would travel to Delphi and see the famous inscription over the temple of Apollo, "Know thyself," each understood the counsel to apply not to himself individually but to himself as a member of the human race. His divinely given task, he thought, was to learn what it meant to be human, in contrast with being a god or a beast. Once he came to "know himself" in that sense, then, he thought, he would know how to live well, keeping to his proper place. The Hebrew

Scriptures evince a similar outlook. They ask, "What is man that thou art mindful of him?" (Ps 8:4).

In contrast, we naturally interpret the inscription at Delphi individualistically. To know oneself, to look for oneself, to find oneself, we think, is somehow to know that which sets each of us, individually, apart from all other human beings. And obviously, if I am viewing others as different from myself, I cannot be wondering what makes all of us the same. For us, it is as if we like to ask, "Who am I, that thou art mindful of me?"

As a result, we spontaneously look at friendships differently. To the ancient mind, to be a friend was to occupy a role. A friend must hold an office. In the friendship between husband and wife, for instance, the husband stands for the male side of the human race in relation to the wife, and the wife conversely, and each conceives of himself as loving not this individual so much as this instance of maleness or of femaleness. Again, two comrades, say close brothers in a family or two soldiers in the field, (who can be as close as brothers), would be conceived of as standing toward each other in the manner of this one instance of manliness alongside this other instance of manliness. But we, in contrast, think of friendships in the first instance as between individuals. These individuals may, for all we know, get bonded together apart from any place they occupy in any natural order—a husband and wife, for all we know, might become bound, on this other way of looking at things, as "soulmates" rather than as this male and this female. As for the brothers or comrades in the field, if they go along with this other way of looking at things (which is harder to do in a large family), they come to think of themselves as bound together, not because they are offspring of the same parents, of the same flesh and blood, but because of something spiritual that likely no one else shares or could appreciate. They may make themselves "blood brothers," but only after they have first established between themselves that they too are "soulmates."

Christianity has played a large role in this change in the concept of friendship. Let's be clear—modern views of soulmates are Christian heresies, although most people do not recognize them as such. But let us consider what a huge difference for the good was made by Christian revelation relative to the classical inheritance. We referred to "the order of grace." This order was understood to complete and save nature, not to negate or destroy it. The role of orthodox Christianity is not to upend the classical conception, but to restore its vitality and give it new resources, power, and extension. But understandably, when Christian concepts get wrested away from their proper role within an economy of salvation as taught by the Church, they can become pernicious and may tend even to subvert the human good.

I shall mention seven new realities under Christianity: (1) the precepts of charity; (2) holiness and heaven; (3) interior life; (4) the importance of the human person as well as human nature; (5) that Christ would give up his life for each one of us; (6) friendship with Christ; and (7) the notion of being sent into the world (apostolate).

(1) *The precepts of charity.* By "precepts of charity" I mean that each Christian is meant to understand his entire life, and all his efforts and striving, as guided by two laws, namely that he love God with his whole heart, soul, strength and mind, and that he love his neighbor as himself (Mt 22:35–40). It follows immediately that to love himself genuinely is to love himself "for the sake of God." What this unusual phrase "for the sake of God" means is that he takes union with God to be his ultimate good, so that he counts nothing as good for him if it is at odds with such union, and nothing as bad if it contributes to this union. Since union with God is holiness, alternatively we can say that, under the precepts of charity, to love

oneself truly is to love holiness for oneself, and to love anything else out of true self-love is to love it only insofar as it contributes to holiness. But this insight has immediate consequences for friendship. If in a friendship each loves the other as himself, then, in the best sort of friendship, each will wish things to another only on condition that they contribute to holiness or at least are not against it.

Thus, immediately the nature of love of a friend has changed. It involves not simply a wishing of good things judged to be good relative to his nature, and his attainment of virtue, but rather relative to his and our own vocation to become holy, with a view to union with God.

(2) *Holiness and heaven.* And this is the second new thing. After self-love has gotten chastened, and its true nature has been corrected, then love of a friend too is assigned a higher ideal. Moreover, the time frame changes by which we evaluate the goods we wish for friends. What each friend now needs to keep in view are matters like, "Are we suited to spend eternal life together?," "Do I truly want him to become such that he can enjoy eternal life, or am I inclined to discount all that?," and "As for myself, do I want to become such that others would find it pleasant and rewarding to spend eternal life with me?" The horizon for Christian friendship is eternity.

(3) *Interior life.* A third reality introduced by Christianity is interior life. Christians regard their relationship with God as prior to everything else. But a relationship with God, the expression of which is prayer, in the first instance is interior and hidden. "God is spirit, and those who worship him must worship in spirit and truth" (Jn 4:24). Jesus tells us to go into our rooms and close the door and pray in secret to Our Father (Mt 6:6). He himself would wake up early and leave the house and town where he was staying to go out to the wilderness to pray, so that his disciples would wonder where he

was and go looking for him (Mk 1:35). He spent many hours, sometimes all night, praying "in secret" (see Lk 6:12–13). St. Augustine in his *Confessions* tells of how surprised he was that his mentor, St. Ambrose, always read silently. Scholars have wondered whether even the practice of reading changed so that it became more like prayer, more like an activity of interior life rather than external action.[1] In any case, clearly, once human life comes to be regarded as interior at its source, then, since strong friends want to have everything in common, it must become part of the ideal of friendship that they share interior life. It becomes a new ideal of friendship that it be heartfelt and sincere. This is an entirely new reality. Conversation, indeed, was always regarded as important for friends. But this conversation was conceived of as directed outward, at external truths. It was not conversation in which each revealed to the other his secret heart. One way of interpreting the chapters in the second half of the Gospel of John is that, because Jesus has pronounced that his disciples are to count as his friends (Jn 15:15), John wants to show clearly what this new practice of Christian friendship looks like.

(4) *The importance of persons as well as nature.* Which brings us to the fourth new reality—the importance of the distinction in persons, as well as the sameness of nature. Christianity holds that God is a Trinity of three Persons each the same in nature, or *homoousios.* (You might find it valuable here to pause and review the Athanasian Creed, to become clearer about how in Christianity we must hold fast to distinguishing the Persons but not dividing the nature.) The *communio* among the Persons of the Trinity, that is to say their friendship, is precisely as Persons of the same

---

1. See *Confessions,* bk. 6, chap. 3. Myles Burnyeat's use of Ptolemy seems to have the opposite upshot from what he intends. But see the whole discussion: "Postscript on Silent Reading," *Classical Quarterly* 47, no. 1 (1997): 74–76.

nature. We perhaps take this truth for granted because we've heard it so often before. (It was a leading truth in the teaching of Pope St. John Paul II.) But we should not lose sight of how unusual it is that there be equal persons in the same nature. Consider the angels, for example. Because angels have no matter, but each is a pure form, it is not possible for two angels of the same form to exist. The reason is that matter is the principle of individuation for creatures that have the same form: there can be two heart-shaped cookies only because each cookie is formed from a different clump of dough; once the dough is taken away, only the form of being heart-shaped is left. Therefore, each angel, a form without matter, is its own species. There can be no two persons who are angels who share exactly the same nature, because angels have no matter that can individuate them.[2] Now, consider that angels are vast in number, vastly more numerous than human beings.[3] Therefore, this vast and magnificent spiritual creation—think of the seraphim, cherubim, and wondrous archangels close to us—contains no two equal persons sharing the same nature. That is to say, in the vast spiritual creation, no angels enjoy the *communio* that is distinctive of the Trinity. However, a *communio* like that is possible for us, because you and I are equal persons of the same nature, and, if we are friends, we share a *communio.* In sum, the introduction of the concept of person in Christianity, to clarify the Trinity, had remarkable implications for how we conceive of human dignity

---

2. My guardian angel differs from yours the way a tiger does from a goldfish, as does yours from the angel of someone else. What saves the angels from being a buzzing blooming mass of confusion is that they are organized into hierarchies. For an angel, an ordinal position in a hierarchy serves to order and locate it in creation, the way a position in a taxonomy does for different creatures which are the same in species.

3. This is the common view of the Fathers and Doctors of the Church.

and human friendship. The locus of dignity in a friendship changes from being centered on a shared human nature to being centered on the persons as much as the nature. A friendship now became not simply a close bonding of different instances of the same nature but also a reciprocal gift of persons, as in the Godhead.

(5) *Christ would give up his life for each one of us.* Now add another new reality, that Christ—God himself—makes it clear that he would die for any one of us (Mt 18:12). Since his gift on the Cross stands for his reciprocal gift of self within the Godhead, he therefore invites each one of us to share in the *communio* of the Trinity (Jn 12:32). This invitation is not only general, to all of us as human creatures, but also addressed to each of us, one-by-one, called by name (Jn 10:27–28). This reality invests the gift of self within friendship with divine significance:

> Indeed, the Lord Jesus, when He prayed to the Father, "that all may be one . . . as we are one" (John 17:21–22) opened up vistas closed to human reason, for He implied a certain likeness between the union of the divine Persons, and the unity of God's sons in truth and charity. This likeness reveals that man, who is the only creature on earth which God willed for itself, cannot fully find himself except through a sincere gift of himself.[4]

(6) *Friendship with Christ.* Prior to the Incarnation, it was impossible for human beings to be friends with God because of the extreme inequality between the Most High and the human creature. But as a consequence of the Incarnation, Christ holds out

---

4. Paul VI, Pastoral Constitution on the Church in the Modern World *Gaudium et spes* (December 7, 1965), no. 24, www.vatican.va.

the offer to be the friend of each one of us (Jn 14:23, 15:15), which implies a new model for being a friend, the model of Christ: "A new commandment I give to you, that you love one another; even as I have loved you, that you also love one another," (Jn 13:34). The new commandment is not to love one's neighbor as oneself but to love one's neighbor as Christ loved us.

(7) *The notion of being sent into the world.* Finally, in the classical understanding of friendship, friendships formed because of nature, human design, or chance. They formed by nature when pairs were drawn to each other because of likeness of age, appearance, or disposition. (Plato's *Lysis* gives a charming depiction of boys who bond in this way.) They formed by human design when parents or governors put people into groups to encourage bonding. They formed randomly if you just happened to encounter someone who became your friend. But in Christianity, there is something new: The Church is itself sent into the world by Christ as Christ was sent by the Father, and each Christian is sent into the world as the Church is sent: "Jesus said to them again, 'Peace be with you. As the Father has sent me, even so I send you'" (Jn 20:21). Christians therefore have a bigger motive for forming friendships and a greater urgency in doing so. In the classical conception, as we shall see next, someone might conclude on many grounds that he needed to form friendships to attain happiness. But in Christianity, we are sent by Christ to form friendships for their eternal good as well as our own.

Christian revelation added tremendous richness to friendship as it was classically understood. The best sort of friendship now became a matter of the common pursuit of holiness, through a sincere sharing of deep matters of the heart, out of a kind of radical abandonment of self for the other, with Christ as a third Person present, in response to whom each was forming and fostering the friendship. What is friendship? Christian friendship is a new creation.

PART 2

The Practice of Christian Friendship

1

The Importance of Friendship: One

Now that we have looked at what friendship is, let us turn to how we, as Christians, form friendships and live friendship well.

All practical matters begin from the end or the purpose for which one is doing something. If the end is important, then, in considering the end, we also remind ourselves of how important that practical matter is that we are considering. This in turn helps us to foster the proper motives. Therefore, the first thing to consider, when considering friendship practically, is why it is important, which will lead us to consider the end.

In this chapter and the next, I want to raise with you several reasons why friendship is important. Some of these are concerned mainly with what we have been calling the "order of nature" and are taken from the classical world. These reasons will be the subject of this section. Others of these are concerned mainly with the "order of grace" and are drawn from Christianity. I will consider these reasons in the next section.

Today, we do not give friendship the importance that is due to it. Socrates used to walk around the marketplace of Athens and challenge his countrymen to live well. He would ask questions such as "Do you eat to live or live to eat?" Of course we should eat to live, but probably most people do the reverse. Take "eating" to stand for relaxation and recreation in general. Then another question becomes, "Do you have fun in order to live better, so that you concentrate on the truly important things, or do you muddle your way through the most important things in order to have fun?" A modern Socrates might ask, concretely: "Do you live for Saturday and 'the weekend,' or do you live for Sunday, to worship God, to offer up your work to him, to spend time with your family, and to render service to the poor?" Socrates's question about food is still pointed. It is still with us today as a broader question about work and rest.

Another question that he liked to ask was simply, "How many friends do you have?" He found that people could not answer this question immediately, or at all. On the other hand, if you asked, "How many oxen do you have?" or "How many houses do you have?" they could tell you right away. This showed either that they did not know what a friend was, or that they cared so little about their friends that they never took the time to count them or took the trouble to test them for genuineness.

We are even worse off than Socrates's countrymen, because they at least lived in a culture where friendship was given some attention by top thinkers in important books. Here is a good place to mention some classical works you might wish to read, to study this topic even better. Plato wrote a dialogue on friendship, already mentioned, called *Lysis*. Aristotle devoted two whole books to friendship (8 and 9) in his great masterpiece, the *Nicomachean Ethics*. Cicero wrote a lengthy dialogue "On Friendship" (Latin, *De amicitia*). But how do we stack up in comparison? For us, without question, the best known and bestselling book ostensibly on the topic, still in print and still selling many thousands of copies each year, is called *How to Win Friends and Influence People.* And yet, this book is mainly about sales techniques.

When Aristotle turned to the question of the importance of friendship, the first thing he said was: "Without friends no one would choose to live." We would say: Life is meaningless unless we live among friends. He probably had in mind all of the social bonds we discussed above, in their variety. But among these, friendship of the best sort is surely indispensable. Let's call this "genuine friendship" from now on—not that the others are false, but that we can easily trick ourselves into thinking, falsely, that the other types are all we need. You can live in the middle of a big city, surrounded by people on all sides, and be desperately lonely nonetheless. You can have enjoyable business relationships with colleagues at work and with counterparties in business, and yet come back to your apartment at night and feel the need to distract yourself because you sense that your life is empty. On the other hand, a husband and wife with a close bond can live, say, in a cabin on the frontier, and, despite unrelenting hardships, they can live a life which seems to them bliss (at least in retrospect). A bleak and hostile environment can be braved with a single genuine friend. Even the death of the other won't render the life of the surviving friend meaningless, because love is stronger than death, and somehow their past relationship carries on in habits and remembrances.

Aristotle also said that we need friends to test whether we have the virtue that is necessary for happiness, and to help us grow in that virtue. You probably know that Aristotle taught that happiness in this world requires that we acquire the virtues and then put them into practice. But what about this project of "acquiring the virtues"? After we've left school, and no one is giving us grades as to whether we've behaved well or not—and, as for assessments at work, if we get them, they are limited and often political—how do we know that we are virtuous? We can't trust our own sense of our own virtue, because we are prone to self-deception, and we like to flatter ourselves. We do not see ourselves as others do. Well, suppose as Aristotle said that virtues make someone good all around. And suppose that goodness is lovable. (As we said, something is good if people are drawn to it, admire it, are fascinated by it, and sense palpably that it is both beneficial to them and enjoyable.) Then, the fact that others like us, enjoy our company, and want to spend time with us—I mean, especially, others with (as far as one can see) good character, who are discerning judges—is pretty good evidence that we have that human goodness that comes from having the virtues.

Robert Burns, the Scottish poet and a great humanist, wrote a poem "To a Louse" which has the famous line, "O wad some Pow'r the giftie gie us / To see oursels as ithers see us!" That's broad Scots for, "We'd be greatly blessed by God if he gave us the ability to see ourselves as others do." But we do acquire this power by friends, by the fact that they stay by us, and by their subtle reactions in our presence. This idea was taken so seriously in the classical world that friends were called mirrors. The reciprocity of friendship was like your image bouncing off a shiny surface, reflected back to you.

But we may need friends even more for the corrections we need for right growth in virtue. By "correction" I do not mean something stylized and deliberate. Indeed, there is something in the Christian tradition called "fraternal correction," in which you deliberately and confidentially draw someone aside and, with charity and humility, express how you believe you were wronged by this person or express your concern about how this person in some matter is not following Christ well. Fraternal correction is very good. But by "correction" I mean simply the constant "micro-corrections" that one gets from spending time with someone who has both human goodness and goodwill toward you. Such a person sets an implicit standard for your own actions and speech, which you will want to live up to. Even in what this person says and avoids saying, you receive lessons about how to see things and about how to act with discretion.

Also, very importantly, this person will not say what you *want* to hear but what you *need* to hear. We should pause and emphasize this point, as it brings up the difference between a "flatterer" and a friend. A flatterer, strictly defined, is someone who says what you want to hear because it pleases you to hear it. A flatterer does not care about the truth, or is willing to ignore or slight the truth, because his goal is not to convey the truth to you but to make your life pleasant. If you have money and power, he may flatter you for base reasons like the ambition of getting ahead in your organization. Or he may be a weak person who wants to avoid at all costs the unpleasantness of saying something unpleasant. Or he may simply not care enough about you to accept the cost—and there is likely to be a short-term cost at least—of telling you the truth. But a genuine friend is invaluable for telling you the truth that you need to hear. If he has virtue himself, he will typically find some inoffensive, probably indirect, soft, and subtle way of telling you. But he'll make sure he gets his point across.

In our own relationships, we must examine ourselves to see that we are not acting like flatterers. Also, we must see that we do not prefer to have flatterers around us rather than genuine friends. St. Pope Leo the Great in his *Gospel Homilies* said that Jesus referred to such a person as a "reed" blown by the wind. St. John the Baptist was definitely not like this. Just as he flattered no one, likewise, he was not in the slightest bit affected by flattery:

> What does the reed represent if not an unspiritual soul? As soon as it is touched by approbation or slander, it turns in every direction. If a slight breeze of approbation comes from someone's mouth, it is cheerful and proud, and it bends completely, so to speak, toward being pleasant; but if a wind of slander comes from the source from which the breeze of praise was coming, it is quickly turned in the opposite direction, toward raving anger. John was no reed, shaken by the wind. No one's pleasant attitude made him agreeable, and no one's anger made him bitter.[1]

And yet how many times have we been let down by others who should have been our friends but ended up being mere flatterers? A flatterer is always a lamentable character and is frequently ridiculous. But sometimes, too, he is disastrous for others. Haven't you heard a woman say, "If just one person had stood by me in that time of crisis, I would not have chosen to have an abortion?" What she means is that no one among those she thought were friends told her the truth: "That is a baby you have conceived, honey. You cannot take it back. You will not be able to live with yourself if you do this. You will have to base your future happiness on a lie." Rather, her supposed friends were flatterers, who said things like: "You can take control of your life. You do not need to have a baby. Doctors say it's a clump of cells. You are right that this shouldn't happen to you. Everything can be made better soon." Indeed, the

---

1. Gregory the Great, *Forty Gospel Homilies*, trans. David Hurst, Cistercian Studies 123 (Cistercian, 1990), p. 30.

difference between friendship and flattery is sometimes the difference between life and death.

We said that friends are important for assuring ourselves that we have acquired virtue, and for correction so that we can grow in virtue. From a human point of view, we want to have the virtues because we want to be happy. Happiness is the goal of this life. It is also the goal of eternal life. There is continuity between the two, but happiness here takes a different form from happiness after death. The biggest difference is that happiness in the next life is contemplative. It is union with God through seeing the face of God, the *beatific vision*. But happiness in this life, which St. Thomas calls "imperfect" happiness, is active as well. It comes from acquiring the virtues and then—this cannot be omitted—putting them into practice well. This leads us to the next consideration, which is that the virtues are best realized and best put into practice among genuine friends, not among lesser types of friendship, and certainly not among strangers.

We get this wrong in our society because of our misguided views identifying "altruism" with love and virtue, and because we set this "altruism" against "egoism." Think of the bumper sticker "Practice random acts of kindness." But all of our actions should show kindness, whereas any random action is likely to be destructive. Virtue is highly refined, like a high degree of skill. Let's take an analogy involving skill, using golf as an example. It would be absurd to say that the full realization of golf skill is to be found in hitting balls at a driving range rather than managing the subtleties of a course like Augusta National in conditions of competition. The former is like virtue exercised among strangers, the latter like virtue put into practice among friends. Or to say that the highest degree of musical skill is shown by an instrumentalist playing in a practice room rather than in a skilled ensemble which has played together for a long time.

Friends do not simply provide the setting in which the refinement of virtue is tested and refined. They also strengthen and magnify the force of virtue in our actions. This is obvious in the case of courage. Stand alongside courageous men and your own courage becomes stronger. But the same is true with all the other virtues. Think of two prudent persons carefully deliberating together, two generous persons inspiring each other to greater generosity, or two humble persons solidifying each other's humility. Think of a time you've been in the company of a truly humble person and tell me whether you felt humbled or not.

Aristotle goes beyond this and says that friends are important for providing what might be called the best "environment" for life. The point may be put this way. We care about our surroundings. We like sunlight streaming into our house. We like fresh air and abundant fresh water. We hang beautiful paintings on our walls and acquire appealing furniture if we can afford it. Moreover, all of these things become even more pleasant if they are familiar, if we know them well, and they carry with them pleasant memories. (This is the love which the Greeks called *storgē* and which C. S. Lewis discusses so well in his book on *The Four Loves*.) Again, we like to have around us photographs, books, and artifacts which express who we are and are tokens of the life we have lived. But if we think in this way about the artifacts that surround us, Aristotle asks, why not even more so about persons? Suppose you acquire over time a good group of genuine friends. You surround yourself, then, with persons who express who you are and are beautiful to look at in both body and soul. They've lived alongside you for many years and bring forward similar memories. They are like you in fundamental ways, and they see things in the same way as you do as a result. Your friends are the best, most beneficial, and most pleasant "environment" for living a good human life. By a similar line of thought, it follows that an even better "environment" would be a large family, related to you by bonds of flesh and blood as well as affection.

I will close this chapter by returning to that maxim of Dionysius, so expressive of the humanity of classical thought, that "love is a unitive and binding force." As we saw, for the ancients, love and friendship were inseparable. You could not even say the word *love* without bringing in friendship, any more than you could explain friendship without appealing to love. The point may be put this way: To say that love is a unitive and binding force is to say that the very purpose of love is to make a bond. Love has a teleology, which is to create bonds. Unless love issues in a bond, it does not bear its intended fruit. But everyone concedes that love is the key to life. "What the world needs now is love sweet love." "All you need is love." "Love and do what you will." "At the end of our life, the only standard by which we will be measured will be whether we loved." And so on. People like to say things like this. Now reinterpret all of these sayings in view of the idea that love is inseparable from friendship, understood as a social bond. And now we get: "What the world needs now is friendships." "All you need is friendship." "Act as a friend in genuine friendships with God and others and do what you will." "At the end of our life the only standard by which we will be measured will be whether we were a good friend." We see that things take a different light. The subjectivity that we are fond of, the freedom from accountability, freedom from commitment and constraint, freedom from correction—all of these disappear, whereas a truthful realism about love now begins to show itself.

In the end, friendship is important for all the reasons that love is important. God is love? God is friendship—which leads next to Christian reasons for the importance of friendship.

2

The Importance of Friendship: Two

As we said, grace completes nature and builds upon nature. Therefore, let us now turn to reasons for the importance of friendship that Christianity adds to those perceptive reasons, so deeply rooted in human nature, that were provided by the classical philosophers.

The first can be stated in the form of a syllogism: A Christian is supposed to imitate Christ; Christ had genuine friends; therefore, a Christian should have genuine friends. It is impossible to imitate Christ without having close friends the way he did. Which close friendships did Christ have? With Lazarus, St. John, and his mother.

We spoke about the inseparable connection between love and friendship. We see this in how these close friends are identified in

Scripture, by reference to Our Lord's love. The love of Our Lord picks out Lazarus as a dear friend:

> When Jesus saw [Mary] weeping, and the Jews who came with her also weeping, he was deeply moved in spirit and troubled; and he said, "Where have you laid him?" They said to him, "Lord, come and see." Jesus wept. So the Jews said, "See how he loved him!" (Jn 11:33–36)

Likewise, St. John the Evangelist is "the disciple whom he loved." Obviously, Our Lord loved all the disciples. This phrase describes a special bond between them.

We said that a mark of friendship is that friends simply want to spend time together, and especially time that they conceive of as "free" from necessity. This is exactly how Our Lord viewed the household in Bethany of Martha, Mary, and Lazarus. He would go there to rest and to refresh himself. St. Josemaría Escrivá, in an extraordinary image, taught that the tabernacle is a continuation of the friendship of this household. We are invited to join this company anytime we wish:

> It's true that I always call our Tabernacle Bethany . . . Become a friend of the Master's friends: Lazarus, Martha, Mary. And then you won't ask me any more why I call our Tabernacle Bethany.[1]

Because the home of Bethany was bound together by the love of friendship, the Church's new memorial on July 29 of Sts. Martha, Mary, and Lazarus is a feast day devoted to Christian friendship:

> In the household of Bethany the Lord Jesus experienced the family spirit and friendship of Martha, Mary and Lazarus,

---

1. Josemaría Escrivá, *The Way* (Scepter Publishers, 2002), no. 322.

> and for this reason the Gospel of John states that he loved them. Martha generously offered him hospitality, Mary listened attentively to his words, and Lazarus promptly emerged from the tomb at the command of the One who humiliated death.[2]

Above I gave the syllogism: We must imitate Christ; but Christ had close friends; therefore, we must have close friends. But we see now how the logic of friendship implies a second syllogism: We must imitate Christ; but Christ was close friends of Lazarus, Martha, Mary, and John; therefore, we too must be close friends of Lazarus, Martha, Mary, and John.

Here is the germ of the idea of the "communion of the saints." An ancient maxim attributed to Pythagoras stated: "The friends of friends are friends."[3] Therefore, any friend of Our Lord is a friend of ours. Therefore, all the saints, who are friends of Christ, are our friends. They are our friends now, while they are in heaven.

A similar reasoning applies preeminently to Our Lady. A friendship is a bond. Therefore, Mary the Mother of Our Lord, who had the closest bond with him, can be called his closest human friend. All of the teachings of the saints about how Our Lord prepared a *mother* for himself in advance, therefore, become equally teachings about how he prepared a *friend* for himself in advance.

So then, a first specifically Christian reason for why friends are important is that the imitation of Christ requires that we have close friendships as he did.

---

2. Robert Sarah, Decree of the Congregation for Divine Worship on the celebration of Saints Martha, Mary, and Lazarus, in the General Roman Calendar (February 2, 2021), www.vatican.va.

3. A mathematician would say that the relation, friendship, defines an "equivalence class."

A second is that holiness is hardly attainable without friendship. A different syllogism expresses this point well: Each of us is called to holiness; holiness cannot be attained without charity; but charity cannot be attained without friendship.

Let's examine this syllogism. Its first premise is that each Christian without exception is called by God to be holy, an ancient truth reaffirmed by the Second Vatican Council:

> The Church, whose mystery is being set forth by this Sacred Synod, is believed to be indefectibly holy. Indeed Christ, the Son of God, who with the Father and the Spirit is praised as "uniquely holy," loved the Church as His bride, delivering Himself up for her. He did this that He might sanctify her. He united her to Himself as His own body and brought it to perfection by the gift of the Holy Spirit for God's glory. Therefore in the Church, everyone whether belonging to the hierarchy, or being cared for by it, is called to holiness, according to the saying of the Apostle: "For this is the will of God, your sanctification." However, this holiness of the Church is unceasingly manifested, and must be manifested, in the fruits of grace which the Spirit produces in the faithful; it is expressed in many ways in individuals, who in their walk of life, tend toward the perfection of charity, thus causing the edification of others. . . .
>
> The Lord Jesus, the divine Teacher and Model of all perfection, preached holiness of life to each and everyone of His disciples of every condition. He Himself stands as the author and consumator of this holiness of life: "Be you therefore perfect, even as your heavenly Father is perfect" (Mt 5:48).[4]

---

4. Paul VI, Dogmatic Constitution on the Church *Lumen gentium* (November 21, 1964), nos. 39–40, www.vatican.va.

The second premise is affirmed also in this passage, because it says that to seek holiness is to "tend toward the perfection of charity."

But then what about the third premise of our syllogism, that charity cannot be perfected without close friendships? Well, first of all, we can say that no one with charity can be like that character described by Fr. Zosima in the *Brothers Karamazov*:

> "I love humanity," he said, "but I wonder at myself. The more I love humanity in general, the less I love man in particular. In my dreams," he said, "I have often come to making enthusiastic schemes for the service of humanity, and perhaps I might actually have faced crucifixion if it had been suddenly necessary; and yet I am incapable of living in the same room with anyone for two days together, as I know by experience. As soon as any one is near me, his personality disturbs my self-complacency and restricts my freedom. In twenty-four hours I begin to hate the best of men: one because he's too long over his dinner; another because he has a cold and keeps on blowing his nose. I become hostile to people the moment they come close to me. But it has always happened that the more I detest men individually the more ardent becomes my love for humanity."[5]

Charity is not loving others in general but rather loving everyone precisely through loving those closest to us. The second precept of charity says, "Love your neighbor as yourself," not "Love everyone as yourself" or "Love others as yourself." How can we claim to love the human being we do not see if we do not love the neighbor we do see? And how can we claim to love another in the fullness

5. Fyodor Dostoyevsky, *The Brothers Karamazov*, trans. Constance Garnett (Modern Library, 1900), p. 64.

of his reality, for who he is, including the faults he carries around with himself, unless we persevere in loving him when he is close to us?

As St. John Henry Newman wrote in his excellent sermon on "Love of Relations and Friends": "The best preparation for loving the world at large, and loving it duly and wisely, is to cultivate an intimate friendship and affection towards those who are immediately about us."[6] Chesterton wrote something similar about one's family:

> The modern writers who have suggested, in a more or less open manner, that the family is a bad institution, have generally confined themselves to suggesting, with much sharpness, bitterness, or pathos, that perhaps the family is not always very congenial. Of course the family is a good institution because it is uncongenial. It is wholesome precisely because it contains so many divergencies and varieties. . . .
>
> . . . The best way that a man could test his readiness to encounter the common variety of mankind would be to climb down a chimney into any house at random, and get on as well as possible with the people inside. And that is essentially what each one of us did on the day that he was born.[7]

Newman also observes that we receive a "training in holiness"[8] by close living with others:

---

6. *Parochial and Plain Sermons*, vol. 2, (Longmans, Green, 1908), sermon 5, pp. 52–53.

7. G. K. Chesterton, *Heretics* (John Lane, 1909), pp. 188–190.

8. "The time has come to re-propose wholeheartedly to everyone this *high standard of ordinary Christian living*: the whole life of the Christian community and of Christian families must lead in this direction. It is also clear however that the paths to holiness are personal and call for a genuine

> Nothing is more likely to engender selfish habits (which is the direct opposite and negation of charity), than independence in our worldly circumstances. Men who have no tie on them, who have no calls on their daily sympathy and tenderness, who have no one's comfort to consult, who can move about as they please, and indulge the love of variety and the restless humours which are so congenial to the minds of most men, are very unfavourably situated for obtaining that heavenly gift, which is described in our Liturgy, as being "the very bond of peace and of all virtues."[9]

And then since charity never fails (1 Cor 13:8)—that is to say, it perseveres—we cannot claim to have charity if we cannot persevere in love toward others in close relationships over time. Over a long period of time, worldly bases for love will change or vanish. Your spouse is no longer youthful or fit; your tastes and interests have changed; dreams were never realized; new challenges and demands have arisen; old resources have vanished. If a friend asks, despite all these changes, "Do you love me as much as before?," charity would be proved if you answered, "Yes, even more than before." Thus Newman asks:

> But what is it that can bind two friends together in intimate converse for a course of years, but the participation in something that is Unchangeable and essentially Good, and what is this but religion? Religious tastes alone are unalterable. The Saints of God continue in one way, while the fashions of the world change; and a faithful indestructible friendship may

---

'*training in holiness*,' adapted to people's needs." John Paul II, Apostolic Letter *Novo millennio ineunte* (January 6, 2001), no. 31, www.vatican.va.

9. Newman, "Love of Relations and Friends," p. 58.

> thus be a test of the parties, so loving each other, having the love of God seated deep in their hearts.[10]

A third Christian reason for the importance of friendship is that friendship is inherently small-scale, and in God's ordinary providence he achieves grand things only from small beginnings. He wants us to work with small things, humbly, having faith that, if it is his will, he will turn small things into big things. Therefore, if we want to participate in that providence, we must foster friendships and cannot have contempt for them.

Sacred Scripture provides many examples of these truths. Jesus was born in a stable. He lived on the periphery of a subjugated and failed people. He was uncredentialed by ordinary human credentialing. Think of how he might have acted. He had divine power: If he wanted, he could have appeared to thousands at once, say, in the Roman Colosseum, with displays of mighty power. He might have made his face appear in the sky, simultaneously to everyone on earth, to give the Sermon on the Mount to everyone. He certainly did not need modern means of communication to communicate to the masses. But he chose a different path. He patiently formed around him a small group of friends, who were weak and fallible human beings with obvious faults and no human distinctions. He sent them out two-by-two as if to say, "You imitate me and do likewise." He taught, tellingly, "Where two or three are gathered in my name, there am I in the midst of them" (Mt 18:20). He might have said, after all, "You will need to fill a stadium with at least a myriad of men (ten thousand) for me to be present; if you can't do that, sorry, I won't be there." But he said, "two or three." When he did deal with a large crowd, feeding five thousand or four thousand men, he did so as if to underline the truth about small things. To

10. "Love of Relations and Friends," p. 59.

steer clear of any misunderstandings, he began with a handful of fish and loaves from a small boy's basket, and he asked the crowd to sit down in small groups.

"Don't forget that, on earth, every big thing has had a small beginning. What is born big is monstrous and dies."[11] If we attempt to be friends with many at once, our affection must become superficial. Today on social media friendship is just mutual "liking" and nothing deeper.

A fourth and final reason why friendship is important for a Christian involves the idea, which we have already seen, that "man, who is the only creature on earth which God willed for itself, cannot fully find himself except through a sincere gift of himself."[12] Can someone make a sincere gift of himself to everyone, or to many, or must it be to a few, or to many through a few?

Jesus gave himself up not simply "for many" but for his disciples right there (Mt 26:27–28). Of course, first of all, before all time, as the Son, he gave himself up to the Father through the Spirit. St. Thérèse of Lisieux is famous for praying for the Church's missions, and one can say that she offered up her life for that intention. And yet at the beginning of her spiritual story we see that her great love was concretized on one particular man about to be executed.[13] St. Maximilian Kolbe's life was one burning sacrifice of zeal for Our Lord and for Mary, and yet he is justly celebrated because he took the place of one particular man in the hunger bunker of Auschwitz. The holy Ulma family did not make a sincere

11. Josemaría Escrivá *The Way*, no. 821.

12. *Gaudium et spes*, 24.

13. Thérèse of Lisieux, *Story of a Soul*, trans. John Clarke, OCD (ICS, 1972), p. 100.

gift of themselves for the persecuted Jews of Poland in general but for these particular Jews whom they sheltered in their farmhouse.[14]

Bl. Don Alvaro del Portillo used to say to a married woman that her path to heaven had a name—the name of her husband—and to the husband that his path had a name—the name of his wife.[15] For a married person there is no general "sincere gift of self" except through a sincere gift to one's spouse, with everything entailed by that. Something similar is true of each of our "neighbors," beginning with those God has made closest to us. Marriage is a natural institution for the ordered and reciprocated conveyance of this gift, but close friendship works in a similar way.

So then, there are at least four reasons why close friendships are important for a Christian: to imitate Christ, as training in holiness, to cooperate with God's providence, and as pathways for making a sincere gift of self.

---

14. See Michael Pakaluk, "'Yes,'" *The Catholic Thing*, September 13, 2023, https://www.thecatholicthing.org/2023/09/13/yes/.

15. Genevieve McCaughan, "Blueprint for a Happy Marriage," Opus Dei, January 3, 2014, https://opusdei.org/en-us/article/blueprint-for-a-happy-marriage/.

3

Marks of Genuine Friendship

Classical thought regards friendship, or "social bonds," as pervasive in society, as we have seen. Christianity, taking all that for granted, goes further and invites us to foster sincere relationships with others, one-by-one, which we have called "close" or "genuine" friendships. So, let's pause and pick out the marks of this kind of friendship. Remember Socrates's question, "How many friends do you have?" The question was hard to answer, in part, because *friend* can mean so many different things. However, once we identify the marks of "genuine" friendship, we can sharpen Socrates's question and ask, more precisely, "How many *genuine* friends do you have?"

Based on what we have said, these marks would be the following:

1. *Stability.* It has everything within it that one looks for in a friendship. Your friend is good in his own right and enjoys life, and he's beneficial to you besides and enjoyable to

be with. And the same holds of him with regards to you. There is no reason within the relationship why it should ever cease.

2. *Sincerity.* In the relationship, there is no "playing of games." Neither friend aims ever to manipulate the other or would even think of it. Neither friend thinks of the other as someone who needs to be "managed." Neither feels any temptation to flatter the other.
3. *Sacrifice.* Each is prepared to give up something of his own so that his friend enjoys the equivalent or better. Each regards his love as shown primarily in what he gives up for the other. (Recall the story "Gift of the Magi.") In the closest friendships, each is prepared to give up his life for his friend (Jn 15:13).
4. *Heart-to-heart.* The relationship tends toward the friends' sharing deep matters of the heart. By this I do not mean "unburdening" the heart, which is something else. (We "unburden" our heart when we tell something to someone that he has no reason to know, in the vain quest to find consolation and peace.) I mean rather that each shares deep aspirations and convictions about the world, and about the good things he enjoys and the bad things he suffers.
5. *Face-to-face.* Genuine friends like to live in each other's presence. They enjoy both looking into the eyes of the other and being looked at: How else can friends be mirrors?[1] One of my sons, when he was eight years old, explained his

---

1. I do not think that C. S. Lewis is quite right when he says, "Lovers are normally face to face absorbed in each other; Friends, side by side, absorbed in some common interest." He's right about absorption, but he overstates his point about posture and attitude. See *The Four Loves* (Bles, 1960), "Friendship," p. 75.

friendship with his best friend: "We sit on swings together and just look in each other's eyes and laugh." Two boys under the summer sun, exulting in being boys and being alive: a great picture of genuine friendship.

6. *Side-by-side.* But genuine friends are not merely face-to-face; they are also side-by-side. And yet they are not so, not, I think, because each "sees the same truth."[2] It is rather that they are stewards and custodians together of some portion of the gift of life that God gives us. With a friend from high school, I am jointly a custodian of "that time" when we were in high school, and what it was like, and what we thought. Two soldiers who remain friends for the rest of their lives are stewards together of all that they suffered in war. A married couple until death parts them are stewards of their time of courtship, and all of the romance in life that was revealed to them then, as well as everything else later.

Review this list, then, and pose to yourself Socrates's question. You may realize you have no genuine friends at all. But, as Socrates also taught, we won't keenly enough desire some very precious good, until we are convinced that we lack it.

2. As Lewis puts it in the same chapter, following Ralph Waldo Emerson.

4

How to Form Genuine Friendships

Suppose that you are a Christian and you realize that you have no genuine friends. How do you go about forming them? Presumably, you *decide* to form them and take reasonable steps. But what about this "decision" that you have made: Does it come from your authority solely, or does your decision affirm what is asked of you, also, on someone else's authority? This question is crucial because the nature of your enterprise, and the resources you have available to you, will depend on it.

Here's an analogy. Suppose I studied all kinds of psychological literature that convinced me that people who show gratitude live subjectively happier lives (which turns out to be true). Accordingly, I "decide" that I need to show more gratitude to others. I realize that my parents would be perhaps the most fitting objects of gratitude, because they brought me into existence, nurtured me, and saw that I got a good education. Therefore, I "decide" to show my parents gratitude—which is all well and good. However, it turns out that, prior to my "decision," God had already commanded me to show gratitude to my parents. After all, the commandment "Honor your father and your mother" includes showing gratitude to them. Thus, what I do in this case, following up on my "decision," is not something I do from my authority solely. When I show gratitude to my parents, I act on God's authority also, because God has previously commanded me, and with his blessing.[1]

For a Christian, friendship is like this. The decision to form friendships is not merely something I may happen to decide, on my own, to improve my life. Friendship is not some kind of "project" or hobby. Friendship for a Christian even goes beyond a necessity relative to our human nature (which it is). Rather, as we have seen, it is something that Christ "sends" us into the world to live out, as his disciples. This is what it means to call friendship an *apostolate*. The word *apostolic* means "being sent." An apostle is a man designated by Christ to be sent on his behalf and with a direct grant of his authority. The Church as a whole is sent. You and I as individual Christians are "sent" by the Lord to practice friendship. When, after pondering all of those weighty reasons that friends are important, we "decide" to seek friendships, our will is simply corresponding to what Christ has already asked of us. "When I speak to you about 'apostolate of friendship,' I mean a *personal* friendship, self-sacrificing and sincere: face to face, heart to heart," says St. Josemaría Escrivá.[2]

---

1. The commandment comes with a blessing attached: "Honor your father and your mother, that your days may be long in the land which the LORD your God gives you," Ex 20:12.

2. Josemaría Escrivá, *Furrow* (Scepter, 2011), no. 191.

Consider the teaching of Vatican II on the apostolate of the laity, which is one of the great glories of the Church. In a crucial passage below, we see that the Church is endorsing the view of human sociability that we have been examining. But it teaches that such sociability for a Christian is a matter of apostolate:

> The apostolate in the social milieu, that is, the effort to infuse a Christian spirit into the mentality, customs, laws, and structures of the community in which one lives, is so much the duty and responsibility of the laity that it can never be performed properly by others. In this area the laity can exercise the apostolate of like toward like. It is here that they complement the testimony of life with the testimony of the word.[3] It is here where they work or practice their profession or study or reside or spend their leisure time or have their companionship that they are more capable of helping their brethren.
>
> The laity fulfill this mission of the Church in the world especially by conforming their lives to their faith so that they become the light of the world as well as by practicing honesty in all their dealings so that they attract all to the love of the true and the good and finally to the Church and to Christ. They fulfill their mission also by fraternal charity which presses them to share in the living conditions, labors, sorrows, and aspirations of their brethren with the result that the hearts of all about them are quietly prepared for the workings of saving grace. Another requisite for the accomplishment of their task is a full consciousness of their role in building up society whereby they strive to perform their

---

3. The council fathers give this footnote: "cf. Pius XI, encyclical 'Quadragesimo Anno,' May 15, 1931: A.A.S. 23 (1931) pp. 225-226. Article 14."

> domestic, social, and professional duties with such Christian generosity that their manner of acting should gradually penetrate the whole world of life and labor.
>
> This apostolate should reach out to all wherever they may be encountered; it should not exclude any spiritual or temporal benefit which they have the ability to confer. True apostles however, are not content with this activity alone but endeavor to announce Christ to their neighbors by means of the spoken word as well. For there are many persons who can hear the Gospel and recognize Christ only through the laity who live near them.[4]

The council fathers go on to distinguish "the individual apostolate" from various corporate or "organized" apostolates. They say that the former "is the origin and condition of the whole lay apostolate, even of the organized type, and it admits of no substitute" (no. 16). In a society in which practicing Catholics are widely dispersed, they say, the individual lay apostolate as involving the practice of friendship acquires a special urgency:

> The individual apostolate has a special field in areas where Catholics are few in number and widely dispersed. Here the laity who engage in the apostolate only as individuals, whether for the reasons already mentioned or for special reasons including those deriving also from their own professional activity, usefully gather into smaller groups for serious conversation without any more formal kind of establishment or organization, so that an indication of the community of the Church is always apparent to others as a true witness

---

4. Paul VI, Decree on the Apostolate of the Laity *Apostolicam actuositatem* (November 18, 1965), no. 13, www.vatican.va.

> of love. In this way, by giving spiritual help to one another through friendship and the communicating of the benefit of their experience, they are trained to overcome the disadvantages of excessively isolated life and activity and to make their apostolate more productive. (no. 17)

Here we come to an important realization. If friendship for a Christian is an apostolate, and we are sent by the Lord, then its very basis must consist of prayer. This insight is explained beautifully in a great spiritual classic, *The Soul of the Apostolate*, by Dom Jean-Baptiste Chautard:

> *Without Me you can do nothing.*[5] This is the principle. The Blood that redeemed us was shed on Calvary. How was God going to insure its fruitfulness at the very start? By a miracle of the diffusion of interior life. There was nothing more paltry than the ideals and the zeal of the apostles before Pentecost. But once the Holy Spirit had transformed them into men of prayer, their preaching began at once to work wonders.[6]

Friendship for a Christian is never merely human friendship but is always a bond which brings along with it at least an opening to the love of Christ. As this love is supernatural, so must the original principle of that friendship have a supernatural basis as well.

I have explained the "apostolate of friendship" for a Christian by beginning with the good of friendship and then moving on to how this good, when infused with supernatural life and grace, can lead unaffectedly to the sharing of the gospel. I proceeded in this way to avoid even the appearance of instrumentalizing friendship. Our task as Christians is not "to form friendships so as to spread the

---

5. "*Sine me nihil potestis facere*" (Jn 15:5).

6. Jean-Baptiste Chautard, *The Soul of the Apostolate* (Image, 1961), p. 115.

gospel." Rather, our task is to form friendships as human creatures. Because we are sons and daughters of God, we practice Christian friendship, which foreseeably, in proportion to the intensity of our interior life and witness, will spread the gospel.

We began this section by asking how we should go about forming genuine friendships. And we see that now our first step should be to pray. We ought to pray because friendship for us must be an overflowing of interior life. We also ought to pray because prayer for us will be the initial expression of goodwill. The first movement of friendship is goodwill, as Aristotle said.[7] We ought to pray for those around us whom we admire and like and would like to become good friends with. We ought to foster the deep goodwill that consists in remembering someone before God, with perseverance, day after day, holding up that person's true good and needs to God in prayer.

The next step in forming friendships is to make ourselves more befriendable. How do we make ourselves attractive, good, and pleasant to others?

Are we pleasant to others? Many of us need to consider our personal appearance. Are we dressed well or do we present ourselves in public like slobs? If I am a woman, do I strive for style rather than sex appeal or trashiness? If I am man, do I look like anyone a woman would want to marry? If you are twenty years old and still wearing sweatpants and a hoodie to class or to meetings, you will look like you have not grown up.

Then there is basic politeness. It is not possible to review everything involved in politeness here. Whole books have been written on the subject. But we should remind ourselves that rules of politeness and manners have arisen precisely as ways of making our

---

7. *Nicomachean Ethics*, 9.5.

dealings with others as inoffensive to them as possible. Manners aim to avoid inflicting anything displeasing to others. They aim to take away any appearance of inflicting anything upon others or coercing them. Consider something so simple as asking, "Pass the salt and pepper, please." "Please" means "If you please." That is to say, "I leave the matter entirely up to you. I would like to use the salt and pepper. If you found it agreeable to pass them to me, I would be grateful." That is to say, with this word, *please*, we have taken something that could have looked coercive ("Do this! Pass it to me!") and turned it into an acknowledgment of the other's freedom to pass it or not. Enjoying freedom is pleasant; being coerced is unpleasant. Such is the nature of manners. Manners also aim to turn animal functions, which could be offensive, into humanized behavior which is stylized and requires art. To grab peas with my fingers and shove them into my mouth is disgusting, because doing so presents the aspect of a brute animal to others at the table. On the other hand, to balance peas on a fork is humanized. It shows skill. Moreover, the use of a fork forces me to take smaller portions. Again, standing up straight, smiling, looking into someone's eyes when we greet them, shaking hands firmly—these are all pleasant, because they display confidence in ourselves and respect for the other.

Most of us need to work on cheerfulness to become more appealing to others. "Sometimes a smile can be the best proof of a spirit of penance"—penance too, which means making the way easier for our fellow brother and sister.[8] Almost any person you encounter in a day will have a dozen reasons to be sad. Can't you make it easier for him, and give him some solace, by showing good humor and cheer?

---

8. Josemaría Escrivá, *Forge* (Scepter, 2011), no. 149.

Men tend to lose cheerfulness because of lingering anger, which spoils their mood, making them surly with others who have no connection with what caused them to be angry. A good example is a father who brings home to his wife and children his anger from some struggle at work. His poor wife and children did nothing to offend him. (But in his anger, he thinks so. The mess of the household, which is understandable and which he should expect, becomes an affront to him which demands immediate and sharp correction.) Women often lose their cheerfulness because their constantly changing bodily condition is a source of frustration. Women are also easily irritated because they do not have thick skins. Men harbor grudges, but women harbor a desire to complain. Complaining to her husband can be a release, but if she has no way to complain, she can remain subdued or sad.

It's not possible to review here all causes of anger or sadness. Besides, each of us has a different temperament, and our circumstances are different. But this is clear: To become more befriendable, you must come to know yourself better and take rational steps to remain cheerful.

We should cultivate activities that help us become befriendable in the ways mentioned. Consider golf as an example. Golf has a dress code which requires that a player look polished and neat. Golf etiquette requires that players take care not to be offensive to others. It effectively asks each fellow competitor to keep in mind always how his own behavior will be viewed by those around him. He must take care to be quiet and not move while others address the ball. On the green, he must mark his ball to take it out of the way. He must not walk across anyone else's line. He must often seek a fellow competitors' consent when he interprets a rule. And so on. Golf is esteemed by accomplished persons for these reasons.

I mentioned not appearing to coerce or impose upon others. The essence of friendship is freedom. Each friend is freely the friend of the other and wishes goods to the other reciprocally in freedom. Freedom requires both "transparency" (in friendship, "sincerity"), and the absence of any kind of physical force. Fraud and deceit, pressure and violence, are opposed to the nature of friendship. Therefore, to make oneself befriendable, one should also take care in one's dealings with others not to relate to them without their knowledgeable consent. Avoid giving orders to others or appearing to give orders. Avoid imposing, pressuring, or bullying, even with slight emotional pressure. Avoid the common flaw of saying something that appears positive but that indirectly gives a criticism, for example, "You are enjoying that dessert a great deal," meant to appear like a positive statement ("You are taking pleasure in what you are doing"), but in reality containing, and felt to contain, a criticism ("You can't control yourself"; "You continue to put on weight").

To be befriendable, not only must you take care to be pleasant or at least not offensive to others, you must also be careful not to give the appearance of being slavish in wanting to please others. You cannot be the sort of person who seems to have no identity of his own and appears to exist for others; who says different things to different persons, because he says what the other expects or wants to hear. You must be what the sociologist David Riesman called (in his bestselling book *The Lonely Crowd*) an "inner directed personality" with his own center of gravity. For this, it helps to develop a solid interior life. Anyone who has strong relationship with Christ will not live to please men.

Besides making yourself more pleasant to others or not offensive, you should address yourself to becoming better through acquiring virtues. There are three kinds of human virtues: virtues of character, which involve controlling the emotions; intellectual virtues, which involve training the mind; and virtues which involve control over the body. Of these, virtues of character cannot be acquired quickly. For someone who is ill-tempered to become mild, for someone who rushes to judgment to become judicious, for someone who is tight-fisted to become generous, for someone who is a slob to become neat—these are all difficult changes, which require much time. They are very difficult to acquire by one's own efforts. Practically speaking, they just about require that you be punished for actions contrary to the virtues and rewarded for actions in accordance with the virtues. That is why drill sergeants are helpful. Sometimes life or nature will do this for us. In any case, you should certainly start working on them right away under the guidance of a spiritual director and with the assistance of grace from the sacraments.

Intellectual virtues as a rule can be acquired more quickly, although not easily. What are intellectual virtues? Knowledge, expertise, skills, and the mastery of techniques and methods. For example, you become very skilled in chess. Or you become an expert in civil war history or macroeconomics or artificial intelligence. In thinking about a skill or expertise to acquire, think about what would be admired by the kind of person you would like to be your friend. Mastery of a violent video game or encyclopedic knowledge of Marvel comics may not attract the kind of person you would most esteem as a friend. If you are in college, when picking elective classes, give some thought to whether the knowledge you can gain in the class will make you more attractive to the sorts of persons you'd like to be your friends.

Finally, you can acquire virtues which involve control over the body. Perhaps you develop great strength in your arms and hands and become a great rock climber. Or you develop endurance and go on long cycling trips. Or you become serious about strength training and bulk up if you are a man or become serious about control and strength if you are a woman and adopt a pilates routine. These bodily strengths will also make you more befriendable because of the toughness and capacity for self-discipline that they signal. Let us not fail to mention in this regard the self-discipline many of us need to exercise to lose weight, so that we get down to a healthy and fit weight.

Then it is important to address deep psychological issues which can be stumbling blocks to frank and unabashed good relations with others. Perhaps you suffer from some secret sin (such as a porn addiction and an addiction of self-abuse) or some secret trauma (suppose you were abused as a child). These will undercut your self-confidence when you are with others. If secretly and silently you are saying to yourself, "I do base things," or "I hate myself for my lack of self-control," you are very likely to repel others implicitly. These deep and secret sources of shame need to be dealt with through sessions with counselors, psychologists, and confessors. They are real and important. You cannot write them off, and you must be prepared to spend money to address them, if necessary, as on any other important good.

In this matter of making yourself befriendable, a final and highly important consideration is to take care in how you speak about some third person when you are with another. Those who are with you will be constantly sizing you up by what you say. If you speak badly about someone who is not present, the person who is with you is likely to wonder, "Will he speak badly about me also, when I'm not with him?" If you reveal a confidence, that person will peg you as someone who cannot keep a secret. If you show disloyalty in your speech, you'll be assessed as a disloyal person. Observe discretion in your speech. Get a catechism and learn the basic injustices we commit against one another in speech and learn to distinguish them—such as backbiting, talebearing, detraction, reviling, and malediction.[9] Bring your day's conversations to your examination of conscience in the evening and be very strict with yourself. Make resolutions for controlling your tongue (see Jas 3:6–8) and ask God's help in keeping them.

Finally, ask the person or persons who know you best what flaws you need to work on and what strengths you should bring out more. Ask your mom or dad, a sibling, a trusted mentor, your current best friend, and your spiritual director. Even ask someone who used to be your friend but you suspect deliberately decided to spend less time with you because of your shortcomings.

While you are doing your best (with prayer and the help of graces too) to make yourself befriendable, you must place yourself in conditions in which friendships form.

Friendships form where activities are such that they elicit friendship-like reciprocal actions from participants. Here are five good examples:

1. *Practices and competitions, rehearsals and performances.* In these types of activity, each person has a part to play and fulfills it reciprocally. Moreover, each person's talents become manifested. Character becomes clear too, not only in how one responds in the heat of the trial (not blaming others, encouraging the best in others, taking on extra burdens) but also in how one speaks during "down time" (saying upbuilding things, being kind and thinking of others, and so on).
2. *Reading groups.* In a good reading group, participants take turns revealing what is in their hearts. Their knowledge and intellectual virtues are revealed. During the reading

9. Or read Thomas Aquinas, *Summa Theologica* 2-2.72–77.

group, they deal with each other face-to-face. If the group lasts, then, while the months and years pass by, they participate side-by-side as custodians of that shared portion of life that was all of those common conversations.

3. *Activism in the service of a noble cause*, such as pro-life activism (clinic counseling, clinic Rosary, marches, organizing speakers' events and debates). These types of activities are good for revealing the noble heart of those who participate in them, because there is no motive for participating in them except idealism. Also, they demonstrate someone's capacity to make sacrifices in the service of the good of others, which, as we have seen, is a trait essential to the best kind of friendship.
4. *Outdoor trips and pilgrimages.* These show our ability to live outside of ourself—not to be preoccupied with ourselves, but rather to appreciate the beauty outside ourselves and think about the needs of others. They can increase our toughness, too, which is similar to a capacity to make sacrifices. Also, the cooperation that these kinds of trips require is a form of reciprocity.
5. *Spiritual activities*, such as retreats, Rosaries, prayer groups, and praise and worship. It requires no little sacrifice to clear time to go on retreat or attend a prayer group. Moreover, few will persevere in a spiritual activity unless they have a genuine love of God, and we have seen that love of God in interior life is the source of friendship.

Next, in any of these activities, if there is someone you'd like to befriend, do a favor for that person or give a gift to him, without being asked and in conditions where there can be no ulterior motive. Don't do anything too extravagant, because that will potentially look servile or officious. But the favor or gift will be a testimony of your goodwill and will be interpreted as such. Moreover, gifts bind. Someone who receives a favor or gift from you will naturally consider himself lightly bound to repay in kind, and then the relationship is on its way to the reciprocity necessary for friendship.

What, then, is the path to forming friendships? Cultivate a life of prayer. Pray for those whom you would like to befriend. Work on presentability, manners, politeness, and cheerfulness. Be gracious and never appear to coerce. Work on acquiring virtues, knowledge, and skills. Deal with secret sources of shame. Avoid indiscretions in speech. Place yourself in conditions where everyone is committed to acting in friend-like ways toward one another. And find ways of doing small favors for others you admire.

5

What Makes Friendship Difficult Today?

Suppose you discover you have no genuine friends. You are prepared to follow the recommendations that I gave in the last section. But you are perplexed and looking for solace: Why does it seem so difficult to make friends today? It helps to understand the current you are swimming against. We can identify four large-scale trends that make it difficult to form and sustain friendships now, for almost all of us, and that predictably will continue to do so into the foreseeable future.

The first is online life. I do not mean primarily doing work online, considered as work. I have written this book entirely while working on a fast computer and using two or three screens or a tablet while on the road. It seems that it makes little difference for friendship whether I read sources on a screen or in a printed book, or whether I write by typing and seeing my words on a screen or type with ink onto paper. And the same seems to hold for other work. Nonetheless, even in doing work on a computer, there is a certain warping of our nature away from its fitness for friendship. The sheer illumination of a screen, with its bright colors and moving images, and possibilities for immediate brief exchanges with others, seems to soak our senses, and give us a sensual consolation, which can make time spent with living persons seem less attractive. Computers and screens of themselves convey a feeling of power and control rather than service. That is why they are so fascinating.

Apart from work, there is the sheer absorption of time by activity on computers and smartphones. When households acquired televisions, people transferred large chunks of their free time each day from social activities, like bowling leagues or card games with friends, to the less social and more passive activity of watching television. This trend has only increased because of computers and smartphones.

Most screen activity is individualistic, even if it seems social virtually. As proof, consider that it makes no difference, as an activity, whether you play chess on your phone with a human partner or play it with a computer. Is the activity truly transactional, or are you manipulating something for an effect? To share a video with someone on a phone is different from watching that video together on a screen. The former leads to two individual watchings, the latter to some kind of shared watching. Screen time obviously fosters self-absorption and encourages tendencies to narcissism. It is crucial that screen time make me feel good. For that, I need a constant obliviousness to my failings. I need to forget that I have anything I urgently need to "work on" in myself. Above all I must believe that I am "liked." The sophisticated companies that make money by fastening you to your screen know all this.

The attitudes mentioned are obviously inconsistent with forming and practicing genuine friendship. That is why it is common to see a group of supposed friends at a table together in a restaurant, and they are not talking with one another, but each is doing something on his phone.

Then, there is the distraction which, when we are with others, interferes with the gift of self to the other that is characteristic of friendship. We have all felt insulted when we were saying something to someone, and in the middle of our sentence, he turns to his phone to look at a notification. The distraction from conversation with God is even more severe. It is an open question whether someone who is continually consulting his phone can "live in the presence of God" as the saints have done. You stop at a traffic light and, instead of remembering your resolution to pray for someone, you check whether you received a new email or a text message. You check the news for the hundredth time that morning or look for an update on the weather when you know the weather hasn't changed. It should trouble us that we can choose these pointless distractions over the opportunity to converse with God. We have seen that interior life is the source of friendship for a Christian. Interior life should be a preeminent good for us such that we ruthlessly exclude competitors.

Another issue is the false mode of sociability that comes from being quasi-anonymous online. The other person is not before you. He is not in your presence to respond to what you say as you are saying it. You do not need to deal with the longer-term consequences of what you say. There is no immediate requirement of politeness. Therefore, you easily become passive-aggressive. You try not to appear completely reprehensible (a "troll"), although you do allow feelings of anger, dismissiveness, disdain, and malice to well up in you. It would be a mistake to suppose that spending two or three hours each day in such a posture does not erode your goodwill toward others when you are not on a screen.

Since smartphones are too valuable and ingenious, they are not likely to disappear, or they will disappear only if something even more ingenious and enticing is invented. Therefore, it becomes essential to a Christian's life of friendship that we practice an *ascesis* (a spiritual discipline) in the use of screens. For example, during Lent, one might give up screen time altogether outside of necessary work. In general, we need to view time on the phone as a low-grade activity—along the lines of watching cartoons on television—and limit it to only a few minutes a day. We must deliberately cultivate activities that crowd out screen time, like board games and reading print books with our family in our living room.

A second trend of today that makes genuine friendship difficult is what might be called the "culture of flattery" which prevails. We can debate what are its causes. Must it arise of necessity within democracies, as some philosophers have held? Is it part of a new phenomenon of "mass society"?[1] Is it a lamentable side effect of the participation of women in public life on a large scale? Does it come from the shift in prosperous nations toward "service economies" where "pleasing the customer" becomes paramount? Is it the result of bad trends in education such as described in Alan Bloom's bestselling book *The Closing of the American Mind*? Is it a consequence of new technologies that favor superficial reactions?[2] The phenomenon does not seem to be passing but looks to be a permanent condition of contemporary life.

But its manifestation is what people call *relativism*. Remember we defined a *flatterer* as someone whose intention is to say what you want to hear and what pleases you to hear. A flatterer will not say the truth if it is displeasing to you. Flattery mimics love; a flatterer

---

1. See Gabriel Marcel, *Man against Mass Society* (Regnery, 1952).

2. See Neil Postman, *Amusing Ourselves to Death* (Viking, 1985).

mimics a friend. Now, consider "relativism." Relativism is the view that nothing is absolutely true, but only relatively true, and that whatever *seems* to be so to a person making a judgment is so relative to him. "Man is the measure of all things," said Protagoras, perhaps the first relativist. From the point of view of getting along with others, relativism seems like a magic potion that renders anything that anyone else says as true. Therefore, you can agree with it. No need to do anything as unpleasant as express that the other person is wrong. You think that there is a right to an abortion? Fine, it is "true for you" that there is right to an abortion. *Voilà!* I can agree with you, even if I believe that abortion is murder, and there is no right to do wrong. My convictions, after all, are only "true for me." Relativism converts all conversation into reciprocal flattery.

If I am right that a culture of flattery is an enduring characteristic of our society, then Christians must learn to get along in it and form genuine friendships nonetheless. How can we do so? We need to become better at disagreeing with others, but pleasantly, through irony, good humor, gentle joking, well-crafted demurrers, and telling stories.

Cultures of flattery turn into cultures of conformity. The reason is that powerful interests often maintain their power through the public assertion of gross lies, which most people probably recognize to be lies but which they don't want to disagree with in order to get along. In our time, powerful interests have promoted the lie that abortion is not killing an equal human being, the lie that two persons of the same sex can be married, and the lie (which goes along with both of these lies), that man and the state can define realities such as life and marriage. In such societies, Christians have always been able to form solid friendships, stronger than death, by meeting in small dissident communities and sharing openly the truths of the Faith. The earliest Christians did so in the catacombs. In communist countries, the Church has had to go "underground." Christians in a heavily secular country probably do well to think of the Church as underground, even if it enjoys the protection of the law and is not being openly persecuted. Christians must understand that they practice their Faith as being among the few honest dissenters who will speak unpleasant truths rather than flatter. They are in the world but not of the world.

A third cultural trend that looks unlikely to go away is broken families. We argued earlier that friendly relations with others are a kind of overflow of interior life. But to say this is to miss a step, because our conception of ourselves is formed in the family. Each child, for example, regards himself as a unity in one flesh of the being of his father and the being of his mother. That is why it is still devastating to a child if his parents divorce after he has grown up. He never stops being the unity in one flesh of the two parents. He would still be torn in two, metaphysically and psychologically, even if his parents were to divorce when he was fifty years old. Therefore, everything goes better in the way of forming friendships if the family is a solid and stable sanctuary. Similarly, everything becomes problematized if the parents divorce.[3]

But we should also add the destructiveness of the sexual revolution, which is a large part of the cause of broken families. If marriage is the closest human social bond, and if sex outside of marriage weakens marriages—it weakens the bond of those who have engaged in sex before marriage, and it weakens marriages generally, in the sense that it coarsens our manners and provides

---

3. Strictly, there is no such thing as a divorce of a valid marriage. I am using *divorce* to mean a separation that the parents regard as irrevocable. Often, one or both of the parents puts a kind of seal on the irrevocability by getting remarried (which, again, is not truly a remarriage, but is concubinage, if the parents were validly married).

constant inducements to infidelity—then, of necessity, the sexual revolution has attacked friendships more generally. The other bonds in a society cannot be stronger than what is by nature its strongest bond. Weaken that strongest bond by insinuating inconstancy and division into marriage, and we can hardly expect that other bonds will flourish.

A fourth reason why it is difficult to form friendships today might be called the stunting of personality or the plague of small-minded personalities. This phenomenon is the other side of the coin of the much-lamented decline of magnanimity in our time. This trend too seems deeply rooted and is likely to be with us for a long time. It arises perhaps in part from mass means of communication, the need of businesses to sell things through pervasive advertisement, the special appeal that frivolity has on screens, the suffocating blanket of secularism which smothers genuine idealism, and the lack of imagination in mass schooling. We see the trend sharply today in concerns everywhere for "safety." We see it too in students' risk aversion. They want to study something that they think will award them with a job right out of school. They dislike the uncertainty of needing to launch as an entrepreneur or sole proprietor.

Here is a list of small-minded concerns (some more valuable than others): what your body looks like; videos of girls posing and dancing; trends in fashion; watching professional sports; accumulating wealth; love of anything you can get only with wealth; what you eat and drink; your clothes; the bills you need to pay; how to earn more money; tourism as entertainment. The list goes on and on, so much so that the really interesting question becomes "What isn't small-minded?" Historically, people have believed that military service to one's country is not small-minded. Building up the Church (think: cathedrals) is not small-minded. Fine art for its own sake and good literature are not small-minded. Traveling for education or pilgrimage is not small-minded. Risk-taking that has some noble purpose is not small-minded (while risk-taking for no noble purpose is small-minded, like wingsuit jumping, despite the appearance of being big). Sleeping around is small-minded; courtship is magnanimous. Owning a dog rather than starting a family is small-minded; generously welcoming children although not knowing how to afford them is magnanimous. Choosing the world yet giving up God is small-minded; giving up the world to follow Christ is magnanimous.

We become small-minded through forms of education that stifle the imagination[4] and suppress children's spontaneous play; by parents who "helicopter" over their children and encourage careerism and résumé building; and by many small choices in a curriculum, such as history that downplays the role of great personalities, bold risk-taking, and decisive events.

A world of small-mindedness is a world hostile to friendship, whereas a world of magnanimous personalities is a world where friendships flourish. In saying this, we simply draw out the social implications of C. S. Lewis's first lecture in *The Abolition of Man*, entitled "Men without Chests."[5]

But what is the basic reason for this association of genuine friendship with magnanimity? It is not unlike that famous line from the *Pensées* of Pascal:

> Man is only a reed, the weakest in nature, but he is a thinking reed. There is no need for the whole universe to take up arms to crush him: a vapor, a drop of water is enough to kill

---

4. See Anthony Esolen, *Ten Ways to Destroy the Imagination of Your Child* (ISI, 2010).

5. C. S. Lewis, *The Abolition of Man* (Macmillan, 1947).

> him. But even if the universe were to crush him, man would still be nobler than his slayer, because he knows that he is dying and the advantage the universe has over him. The universe knows none of this.
>
> Thus all our dignity consists in thought. It is on thought that we must depend for our recovery, not on space and time, which we could never fill. Let us then strive to think well; that is the basic principle of morality.[6]

It is a wonderful passage. Yet we can add that man is more than a *thinking* reed: He is also a reed with a heart, whose dignity is shown too in what he chooses and clings to over other things. In a genuine friendship, which of itself lasts forever, a man asserts his own eternal dignity in choosing with his heart the dignity of his friend and of their bond over everything that exists merely in space and time. In this there is true greatness: "I have said this to you, that in me you may have peace. In the world you have tribulation; but be of good cheer, I have overcome the world," (Jn 16:33).

---

6. Blaise Pascal, *Pensées*, trans. A. J. Krailsheimer (Penguin, 1966), no. 200, p. 95.

6

Some Particular Advice About Friendships Once Formed

Suppose you have formed a genuine friendship. But how can we tell when a friendship is no longer *forming* but has already *formed?* Aristotle wondered about this. He said it takes a while for a genuine friendship to form. Two persons can quickly want to be friends and want to become friends quickly, but friendship is objective, regardless of what they want. Genuine friendship requires a solid insight into the goodness of another person, solid trust in the other, and a general steadiness in standing by the other, and all of this takes time. A friendship is not an emotion but an enduring trait in each of the friends, similar to a virtue, together with a "structure" in the friends together. As we said, it is more like an institution than a feeling, and sometimes is an institution, like marriage.

The Greeks had a proverb to express these ideas, "a bushel of salt." Goethe in a poem has one of his characters explain:

> Often appearances cheat; I like not to trust to externals.
> For I have oft seen put to the test the truth of the proverb:
> Till thou a bushel of salt with a new acquaintance hast eaten,
> Be not too ready to trust him; for time alone renders thee certain
> How ye shall fare with each other, and how well your friendship shall prosper.
> Let us then rather at first make inquiries among the good people
> By whom the maiden is known, and who can inform us about her.[1]

There are 7,150 teaspoons in a bushel. Suppose two persons cook together and use between them four teaspoons per day. They would need to spend almost five years to go through a bushel of salt together.

But Goethe points out something very important, which is that our enjoying the good opinion of people we trust, and having a reliable background (such as coming from a good family), can do a lot of the work of direct experience. A sincere profession of religious truths can also speed up the process. Often, on such foundations, a man and a woman in just a couple of weeks can come to know each other well enough to be responsibly married.

Many writers on friendship say that it's possible to test whether a friendship has formed. To find out whether someone is trustworthy, for example, tell him something confidential, which is not very important, but which would be tempting for someone to

---

1. From his epic poem *Hermann and Dorothea*, under the section, "Clio." Trans. Ellen Frothingham. (Boston: Roberts, 1879), pp. 101–102.

reveal to others. If this person does reveal it, then you know he's not trustworthy: He is not a genuine friend and is probably incapable of ever becoming one.

Another test is whether someone continues to trust you against allegations and evidence to the contrary. If he suspects you of revealing a confidence or speaking against him or betraying him, he gives clear evidence that he does not trust you and therefore is not a genuine friend.

Another test is how a person behaves and speaks about you when not with you. If he speaks badly about you, then he is not a friend.

In general, a friend's willingness, just on his own, to accept a substantial burden, just for you, without any expectation of an immediate quid pro quo, will be a sign of a formed friendship—because he assumes, as do you, that there will be reciprocity in the long term over an indefinite future. He is taking for granted that the relationship will continue indefinitely.[2]

As regards the specific friendship between man and woman that is marriage, it was traditionally regarded, with good reasons, that the "intentions" of the man in particular could be tested through in his behavior in courtship. If he insisted on sexual favors or made it seem that he would leave if he did not receive them, or if he pressed himself upon the woman, then that was sufficient evidence that he did not love her for who she was but for what he could enjoy. Chastity in courtship, despite often strong inclinations

---

2. We have to say, "just on his own" and "just for you" because, say, if the men from the town come over to help you raise a barn, which is a substantial burden on each, they act corporately rather than individually. It is a kind of civic friendship which they display. They act on the general principle that "We should help anyone among us raise a barn."

to the contrary, is the best evidence that the man and woman are on the path to a genuine friendship.

In general, because a friendship is a "state" or enduring trait rather than an emotion, then anything that testifies to the presence of a "state" testifies to the reality of the friendship. For example, if you wish to spend time with another regardless of your mood, that is a sign of an enduring state. If you and the other can get along with each other well, even though a lot of time has passed since you were last together, then that is the sign of an enduring state (just like you never forget how to ride a bike). If out of the blue the person asks a favor of you and you are prepared to drop everything to do it, that is the sign of a state. If each of you is equally disposed to get in touch with the other for spending time together, and it is not lopsided and one person's initiative mainly, then that is the sign of a state.

But now let us assume that you are assured that you have formed a genuine friendship. What advice should you keep in mind? This is the question of how we should act toward friends. It ought to be obvious what we should do, but our culture has little clarity about it.

First, you should try to live near your friends, since friendship is so valuable, and we can easily spend time only with those we live near. However much we think we can transcend this rule, we cannot. It is practically necessary that you live in the same neighborhood as your friend. At the very least, you cannot live farther away than, say the same drive we make to commute. We show whether we esteem our friends as we should by how much living near them counts for us in decisions about education, jobs and location. At the very least, they should be consulted when we make such decisions, and we should not move away from them unless they agree that all things considered the move makes sense.

Second, whether we live nearby or not, it is necessary to maintain a friendship by regularly communicating with a friend. Aristotle in this connection cites the proverb "Many a friendship has been lost for lack of a greeting." Friendship is a "state" and like any other state needs to be exercised.[3] Here is one undeniable good role for social media in friendship: It does help friends who live apart stay in touch. Even so, a post on social media sent out to all of your "followers" is far inferior to a personal communication by voice. In these matters, personal communication is better than general communication and voice is better than writing. Women see this more easily than men. Women will hold their friends and husbands to the standard of conversing, even if only briefly, at least once a day. Men, in contrast, will hardly wish to communicate unless there is some felt "cause." And yet, they should correct themselves and more frequently call a friend even without a distinct reason. Your friend may at first be surprised to be called "out of the blue," and yet he will come to see the goodness of it and likely reciprocate. (But if he never does, you may need to scale back, because there must be equality in a friendship. Friends will make it clear just how close they want a friendship to be.) Some people make themselves too busy to maintain their friendships. Worldly cares and anxieties can choke off friendship just as they choke off the gospel.

Third, over time, various shortcomings in your friend will become more apparent, and these may become quite irksome if you live near your friend or otherwise spend much time with him—say, your families go on vacation together.

In such cases, great patience is necessary. Many of us take many years to overcome shortcomings; a friend is supposed to help

---

3. Because persons, intentions, and feelings are in play, a friendship needs to be "kept" in the way a habit like bike riding does not.

in this, not be a source of complaints. Realism about the human condition is necessary too: Sometimes God wishes that we deal even over our whole lives with a shortcoming, say, to teach us humility and the need to rely on his graces. What you see in your friend is in you also, probably in a different form. Perhaps the most difficult spiritual work of mercy is forbearance of the shortcomings of others. You gain a lot of merit every time you hold your tongue or smile instead of complain. "Don't say: 'That person gets on my nerves.' Think: 'That person sanctifies me.'"[4]

We have already discussed fraternal correction, which has its place—but it must be well justified, deliberate, used sparingly, and not given more than once for the same shortcoming. It is necessary to add this: Because of the equality of friendship, be wary of giving a fraternal correction to a friend if it is plain that he will never reciprocate by correcting you. If you act as though you are superior to your friend, then you are no longer a friend.

Fourth, keep politics in a distant second place to other interests in your friendship. By "politics" I mean "how prudentially it is best to love your country." In contrast, "religion," understood as how to love and serve God, cannot be secondary. If there are differences in religion between you and your friend, the soundness of your friendship requires not that you ignore these, but rather that you both understand that, through your friendship, God wishes whichever of you has the truth, or the fuller truth, to lead the other friend to that truth.

Obviously, God is our highest good and the truth about him can never be secondary. But the well-being of our country, although higher than the individual good of any citizen, is not our highest good. In fact, it is passing, like all worldly goods. Yet

---

4. Josemaría Escrivá *The Way*, no. 174.

our passions about politics may be strong. Therefore, we may need deliberately to mortify them. Keep in mind that apart from matters of natural justice, political questions fall within the realm of the free operation of prudence, where we ought to expect that persons of goodwill will reach different conclusions. If such differences cannot be patiently worked out in the context of a genuine friendship to achieve mutual understanding, then where can they ever be worked out? It is the purpose of a genuine friendship to achieve what public discourse does not so easily achieve.

Fifth and finally, there is the question of how to deal with a friend who was a genuine friend but then goes astray. Let us take an extreme but not uncommon example. You and your friend were very close in the practice of the Catholic Faith and in working on various good causes together. But he has a "midlife crisis," abandons his wife and children, and runs off with his secretary. He even claims he is no longer married to his wife and starts a family with his secretary. What then? You will face two conflicting considerations. One is the understandable wish to punish his behavior socially by shunning him. The other is the sense of loyalty, and gratitude for all the good things he did for you in the past as your friend, and so you will hope and pray that he finds the right path again. You will believe that as his friend you are likely to have some role to play in helping him do that.

The pagan Aristotle long ago opined that in such situations, so long as there seems a chance that his life and character can be saved, and there is no danger that he will draw you along with him into a collapse like his own, then you should continue to be a good friend to him, doing what you can. There will no longer be the best kind of reciprocity in the friendship. But you should conceive of your continuing friendliness to him as reciprocating for his past good services to you. It seems to me that this advice is sound, except one needs to add that you should never act in a way that causes scandal, that is, that signals or implicitly communicates to others the false message that you approve of what your friend has done.

Christians have an additional motive to follow Aristotle's advice: They are followers of the Good Shepherd who explicitly taught that he leaves the ninety-nine safe sheep to look for the one lost sheep. But for all that, very strong emotions can come into play in these matters, and it simply may not be humanly possible to put them aside. Suppose, in the case I just gave, you are very close to the wife and children and share in their feelings of betrayal and abandonment. You yourself are hurt with their hurt; you yourself feel the anger of injustice which they feel. You can no more negate these feeling than can they. If so, then your spontaneous humanity, and the state of your heart, may render it impossible for you to continue to act in a friendly manner toward your former friend. It is not that you decide deliberately to shun him but rather that you find yourself overwhelmed with pain and revulsion. You continue to pray for him: This is all that you find yourself able to do.

It is not possible to reach any general judgments in difficult cases like these. The safest course for you will be to seek the counsel of a good spiritual director and follow it.

There are differences between the friendships of men and those of women. These differences arise from the interplay of the different natures of men and women and how different cultures express these different natures. For example, it is of the nature of a man to want instinctively to serve and to protect. In the United States, therefore, where there is a culture of the peaceful use of firearms, it is distinctive of men to know about, collect, and practice using firearms. Nothing, of course, prevents women from doing these things, but understandably they are not drawn to it in the same way. Thus, friendships among men often bring in the use of firearms somehow, for example, when men go to a shooting range together. But in other societies where there is no such culture of the peaceful use of firearms, friendships among men find other expressions. In England, for instance, there was a tradition of men gathering in public houses after work to enjoy time just among themselves before heading home to be with their wives and children. Understandably the picture of men by a roaring fire, smoking their pipes, with their shoes off to let their feet dry, came to stand for the distinctive friendship of men. C. S. Lewis's exposition of friendship in *The Four Loves* is highly influenced by this picture. His own experiences among his group of writer friends, the "Inklings," confirmed it. He disclaims in his chapter any idea of what distinctively female friendship is like.

It is not easy to say much that is concrete and lasting about these differences between men and women's friendships. Lewis's picture is already out of date in England. However, we can say this: The Christian laity in general are placed in a position of stewardship over the good things of God's creation. This stewardship extends to the distinctive charisms of being male or female. Therefore, in how we educate children, how we set up the work environment, and how we practice friendship, we need to be sensitive to these differences and aim to protect and amplify them in reasonable ways. Hence, two male friends need to keep in mind, "What are the characteristic ways for men, as men, to be friends in this culture and time?"—that is, what ways can they endorse as consistent with Christianity—and aim to realize this in their friendship. Two female friends should do the same. Often, one of the men is "not as manly as he should be," or maybe both are not, and similarly as regards women. In these cases, the vehicle of friendship, which we have seen is so naturally useful for so many other goods, helps us to live better our God-given vocation to serve Christ specifically as a man and specifically as a woman. Friendship over time should help men become more manly and women more womanly.

One further point should be made in connection with maintaining friendships: We should take care to observe what is called the "order of love" (*ordo amoris*) or "order of charity" (*ordo caritatis*). By these phrases two distinct things are meant. Sometimes, it is meant that four basic realities should be loved in a certain order: God before one's own soul; one's own soul before a neighbor's; and a neighbor's soul before one's own body. This ordering represents what one should be prepared to sacrifice for what. I should be prepared to sacrifice my soul, that is, my life, for God—in martyrdom, if he asks of it. I should not be prepared to sacrifice my soul for my neighbor's benefit. But I should be prepared to offer up my body, or rather goods corresponding to the body, for my neighbor's ultimate good. (That is why we say that property should be privately held but directed in its use to the common good. This is just the principle that, in general, each of us should regard goods of the body as properly ordered to the welfare of others.)

But more frequently by "order of love" what is meant is that, as St. Thomas says following Aristotle, we should typically show more love to those closer to us and more love to those who because of holiness are closer to God. (These two considerations can obviously work against each other.)

The point to make here is that friendships will not be practiced well, and will be at risk of breaking down from excess or defect, if we do not observe the order of charity. The chief way in which people get this wrong is by neglecting their brothers and sisters by blood in favor of friends who were originally strangers. Another flaw occurs when because of the fascination of a new friend we neglect or even show contempt for an old friend—for example, when we move to a new city for a first job and neglect our friends back home from childhood and high school.

It is not Christian to love all persons with the same degree of active love. The view that we should do so is sometimes called *liberalism* or *globalism* and is recognized to be a tendency that subverts families, neighborhoods, and countries. Indeed, what people call the "thanatos syndrome," an apparent death-wish within "liberal" cultures and civilizations, is most often a failure to observe the order of love.

7

Friendship Between Husband and Wife

I will close this book by discussing two important friendships for married Christians: the friendship between a husband and a wife, and the friendship of husband and wife with their children. The first is a condition of the second: The parents can hardly expect separately to become friends with their adult children if they do not have a good friendship between themselves.

It must be understood that a family is a community of three communities. The bond between the husband and wife is the first community of a family and its foundation. Then, there is the community of the parents with the children. Finally, there is the community of the children among themselves. Newly married couples, obviously, see and understand that they are the first community of their newly formed family. (Yes, a married couple is a family already.) However, it often happens, if they are generous and self-sacrificing, that they throw themselves into raising their children to the neglect of their original bond. Tending to "their" relationship can even begin to appear to be a self-indulgent luxury. Nothing can be further from the truth, because, again, their marriage is the foundational community of the whole enterprise.

Corresponding to these three natural communities are three natural structures of authority. Aristotle perceptively pointed out that all three forms of political authority (monarchy, aristocracy, and ordered democracy[1]) are inherent by nature in the family, and therefore the family is the source of all political order in society. The father is the head of the unity composed of the three communities. "The husband is the chief of the family," says Pope Leo XIII, in his great encyclical on Christian marriage, *Arcanum divinae sapientiae*.[2] "For if the man is the head, the woman is the heart, and as he occupies the chief place in ruling, so she may and ought to claim for herself the chief place in love," says Pope Pius XI in *Casti connubii*.[3] The mother and father together operate as an aristocracy, as shown in the fact that they divide up the household into different "domains." If they have a good relationship, each respects the authority of the other in that other's domain, deferring to the judgment of the other. The children constitute an ordered democracy insofar as, on the one hand, each child "has

---

1. Aristotle and many of the ancients regarded "democracy" as a corrupt form of government. It was inherently irrational, because why should multiplying the number of persons holding a foolish view give that foolish view more weight? They would use instead a term like *timocracy*, which is roughly the rule of the many based on experience and good judgment. We can call it "ordered democracy."

2. Leo XIII, Encyclical on Christian Marriage *Arcanum* (February 10, 1880), no. 11, www.vatican.va.

3. Pius XI, Encyclical on Christian Marriage *Casti connubii* (December 31, 1930), no. 27, www.vatican.va.

an equal say," and, on the other hand, the older child on the scene enjoys a temporary higher authority and often makes decisions *in loco parentis*.

Despite modern attempts to reengineer the family, mainly to make people feel better about broken families by saying, "That's okay, there are many types of family,"[4] this teaching of Aristotle, which was followed by St. Thomas and reiterated by the popes, seems in outline correct, and happy families intuitively follow it. The relevance to friendship is this: Only the friendship among equal companions or siblings of roughly the same age is equal in its structure. Only in this kind of relationship will the friends retain a friendly aspect to each other precisely by striving to maintain an ideal of equality. All other friendships have some kind of structure of authority, natural or acquired, which corresponds to some kind of inequality. The bonds of these friendships cannot be strong unless the nature of this authority is at least intuitively recognized and guides how the persons relate to each other. For example, what is "friendly" behavior between husband and wife in the running of the household? It is friendly for the husband to recognize that the wife has her own "domain" and to defer to her judgment (often against his own judgment) in that domain; it is unfriendly for him aggressively to ignore that she has her own "domain" or to overrule her without strong necessity in her domain. Again, obviously, parents are not equal to their children. If parents treat their children as their "buddies," the children become spoiled; they learn to manipulate the parents as if they were in control instead; and the result is a disaster. The social bond of parents with children requires that children recognize the authority of the parents and honor them.

---

4. Another example of the "culture of flattery" in which we live.

As regards the friendship which husband and wife have, not in the running of a household, but specifically as partners potentially in procreation, it is not our purpose here to review the Church's rich teaching on chaste wedlock. For that, you might start with the magnificent encyclical on marriage just mentioned. Here, we simply consider marriage as a friendship and look at marriage under that one aspect only. Our task is to take the theory and practice of friendship in general, already reviewed, and see what is distinctive about this highly important social bond which is marriage.

First, let us consider how marriage forms. In non-Christian cultures, marriages are either arranged, or they are a side effect of sexual relations. If the latter, people are prepared to sleep around and if, for convenience or because of strong emotions, they cohabit with one sexual partner, they may eventually seek to formalize that relationship. Our own culture insofar as it has reverted to paganism is like this. However, add for our culture that people also deceive themselves, retaining an ungrounded idealism about marriage. They often suppose that sex will of itself lead to marriage, when it does not.

But marriage in Christian cultures is conceived of differently. Marriage itself is regarded as a mystery which represents the mystery of the Incarnation (Eph 5:32). As Christ joined himself to human nature when he became man to win the Church as his bride, so man is joined to woman antecedently through the "nuptial meaning" of his body, and a particular man, acting in accordance with this meaning, will seek a woman as his bride in a one-flesh unity. Just as the Incarnation took place among the Jewish people only after centuries of covenants, by which God proposed a special relationship with his chosen people, so the ideal of Christian marriage is that it follow upon an extended pursuit by the man of the consent of the woman.[5] Everything which we call "romance" derives ultimately from the relationship of Christ with the Church.

Marriage, unlike other forms of friendship, can form quickly, as we said. It sometimes happens that two persons know within moments after they first meet that they want to get married; they shorten engagement as much as possible; and they live together as husband and wife for decades until one of them dies. This sort of thing is possible because the relationship of marriage is, as it were, foreordained by nature and grace. It is not unlike this: A tiny baby boy is brought home from the hospital and everyone in the family, all his older brothers and sisters, immediately fall in love with him and "know" that they will be faithful friends with this creature for the rest of their lives. There is no need for any "bushel of salt" to confirm the relationship. Similarly, because of the "nuptial meaning of the body," there is something antecedently existing, a "natural institution," raised by Christ to a splendid sign and instrument of grace. The husband and wife, when they get married, are assuming roles *that have already been marked out*. This is why the myth of "soulmates" is so pernicious, because it detracts from the power inherent in the institution. There are no soul mates, ever: There is this man, and this woman, and a natural institution, which is a preordained mode of union. They are bound by this institution, not by any putative, mythical ordination of the soul of each for each.

We said that a friendship is realized by a reciprocal wishing of goods similar to those by which the friendship was first formed. If so, then we must understand the bond of marriage as a continuation of courtship. Just as politics is war by other means, marriage is

---

5. How concretely the concept of courtship became more fully developed in the Christian West is explored wonderfully by C. S. Lewis in his greatest work of scholarship, *The Allegory of Love*.

courtship by other means. Courtship is like a dance: It is a drama through which each person, the man playing a role that represents protecting and serving, with strength, and the woman playing a role that represents making a hearth and home, with softness, consents to make a donation of one's whole life to the other, not holding anything back, so that the other person becomes this person's path to God, such that each one's own eternal destiny hinges on each one's fidelity to the solemn promises of the relationship. To get married after this dance or drama is to burn the bridges behind you and burn the evacuation ships on the shore. It is an act of extreme risk and a complete adventure. At the wedding ceremony, the couple bring everything they have; they have nothing left to hand over. Everything is wagered on the marriage.[6]

Therefore, a marriage must be just like this each day also, not as dramatically as at the wedding, but at least symbolically so. Of course, it can sometimes be so in a very dramatic fashion. It is so when the mother is pregnant and giving birth, or the father is (say) building a house for the family, pouring out his blood, sweat, and tears under the hot sun. It is so during any act of sexual intercourse (more about this in a moment). But it is so less dramatically yet still symbolically in, say, how husband and wife say please and thank you, neither taking the other for granted. Or in how they together conceive of the daily contribution of each to the household. Or in how they take little favors or inconveniences on behalf of the other to stand for how each has given completely of himself to the other.

In *A Severe Mercy*, Sheldon and Davy Vanauken expressed this last point with a saying, "A cup of water in the night." That is to say, "I will bring you a cup of water in the night anytime you ask for it. It will never be an inconvenience. And, although it is a

---

6. This is why "prenuptial agreements" render a marriage invalid.

small thing, the cup stands for all of my love." In the romance of a Christian marriage, the man's taking out the garbage before it is overflowing, before anyone needs to point it out or ask, is an act of the highest gallantry. Who needs to slay dragons if the garbage is there to take out? The woman's taking care to get up long before her body says that she should, to make a hot breakfast for her husband before he leaves for work—no damsel in a castle was ever more worth winning.

I mentioned that in the marital embrace, too, all ships must be burned. So burn them. Place yourself in peril and at risk. Make a wager with an eternal payoff, that a new immortal being will come into existence here and now. From what might easily be just a reenactment of the function of brute animals, turn your act, with its risk and boldness and faith, into an act of everlasting merit, and a participation in the divine.

We are talking about a mistake like what Protestants make about the Eucharist. When Our Lord says, "Do this in remembrance of me," they think "this" must be a "a mere symbol" and not the same reality again. But the "this" which Our Lord wants us to do, again and again, is to make him present as he made himself present in the bread and wine at that Last Supper. Likewise, the "this" which a married couple does in the marital embrace is not "a mere symbol" of their marriage. We don't overstate if we say, "It is their marriage." Or, with greater precision, we can put the matter thus: They "say" in the way they structure their marital embrace what they think their marriage is.

St. Pope John Paul II in *Love and Responsibility* and his *Theology of the Body* argued not that the procreative dimension of intercourse "should not" be separated from the unitive, but rather that it "cannot." Remove the one and you remove the other. We can translate the point into the Aristotelian terms of "complete" or "perfect" friendship. In a complete friendship, as we saw, each friend is beneficial to the other and enjoyable because of the good that is within the other. That good is seen, and loved, and we wish goods to the other on account of that good, but because goodness is inherently linked to usefulness and pleasure, we gain—in the manner of consequences—usefulness and pleasure as well in the relationship. In a marriage, the husband (we'll take just this case) sees the goodness of the woman, as a woman, which includes how she is created by God to make a home and has the power to conceive children within her, and if he loves her, that is, marries her, on that basis, then he enjoys as a consequence say, the hot breakfast she makes for him (a useful good) and her smile and feminine appearance (a pleasant good), and even the warmth of her body and the pleasures of her embrace. But if he comes to regard her power to conceive as bad, then he no longer sees or endorses the relevant good that is within her, and therefore, to that extent, he converts his relationship with her to one of mere use. Their bond becomes "a coincidence of egoisms," as John Paul II said. Moreover, since how they structure the marital acts "says" what they think their marriage is, they convert their marriage itself to a coincidence of egoisms, no greater, as a bond, than the relationship of the butcher and baker. Maybe the marriage itself can survive this misrepresentation, by the custodians of that bond, of the nature of that bond. But what they do corrupts the marriage while they do it and tears down something holy.

Because husband and wife occupy "offices" in a natural institution, raised to a sacrament, they have a fiduciary responsibility. It is their responsibility to deliberate about the state of their marriage on a regular basis, to take stock of where they are and where they are going. They are obliged to make diagnoses about what matters need correction and improvement and together to make resolutions to deal with them. They need to revisit these resolutions and see whether changes are necessary or perhaps were successful. They need to exercise a kind of pastoral care over all three communities in their household, besides giving particular thought, one-by-one, to each of their children, in all dimensions of human development: health, education, spiritual and religious, and social. In short, they need to give no less attention—and probably more—than they would give to a business they were founding. They are the chairmen of the board, trustees, CEO, CFO, and COO, all together, of their marriage.

This discharge of their fiduciary responsibility takes time. If we say that a marriage is an institution, we must treat it like an institution. In my experience, a married couple does best to get away on a kind of marriage retreat lasting at least two days on preferably an annual basis. Call this an "off site," if you wish, using the language of businesses. My wife and I have used the language of "navigator's conference," which we took from *A Severe Mercy*, because husband and wife are as if officers of a boat, who are charged with bringing the boat, themselves, and the passengers all safely to port.

Many couples with young children will consider that a retreat like that is a luxury which they cannot afford. To this I say three things. First, families on a very austere budget nonetheless do find ways of coping with genuine necessities. The front end of that old car you are nursing along breaks down, and you must find a way to repair it. And you do. The water heater breaks: You get it replaced. And so on. Second, there are always inexpensive substitute ways of doing things. A friend has a second house that he will let you use if you explain that it is for a necessary, good cause. Or you do something like a "stay-cation" by asking grandparents to watch the children, and your "getaway" is simply a long day trip to a local park or beach. Or you find another couple who recognizes the need for regular marriage retreats and you agree to reciprocate in watching each others' children for a day or two. Third, I am assuming that even if your budget is very austere, you are still giving money away and perhaps even aiming to tithe. Discuss the matter with a spiritual director but, in my opinion, a regular marriage retreat, just like a spiritual retreat, is so important that spending money on it, in a moderate way, can if necessary be counted as alms—because all the other good that you do for your children, your parish, your community, and society at large depends upon the strength of your marriage.

Couples who embark on a marriage retreat for the first time are likely to be rather stylized about it, understandably so, because they are doing so with a consciousness of their responsibilities and want to make good use of their time. As an appendix to this book, I provide simply as an example the advice on holding the navigator's conference which my wife and I composed early in our marriage. We are much more informal now, after twenty years. But the basic idea of a marriage retreat is easy to state. As in everything else, there is on the one hand the "ideal" and then, on the other hand, there is the "workable ideal in the circumstances," and we must settle for the latter.

Length. Ideally, your retreat should be two full days and three nights, something like this: You arrive one evening, spend the first full day "decompressing," and spend the second day conferring, after which you have a romantic dinner and leave the next morning. But minimally, it should be one full day.

Place. Ideally, your retreat should be at a place of calm and natural beauty to aid in giving distance, clarity, and perspective. Minimally, it should be in some spot free from the distractions and cares of the household.

Schedule. You should compose and agree upon a schedule that allows time for daily Mass, prayer, and the Rosary. Ideally, you should include time for a walk or some kind of exercise together. Ideally, six or seven full hours should be devoted to conferring, but minimally around four.

Topics. You should agree in advance on what needs to be discussed and divide up the time so that you give due attention to each topic. Try not to leave out anything of importance. For example, you might discuss:

a. Your spiritual life: Both how you are progressing individually (and how the other can help) and practices within the family like prayer, going to Church, and the Rosary.
b. Your marriage itself: How it is faring, what needs to be improved, how problems should be addressed.
c. The children: Consider them together and then each separately, discussing the education, character development, and health of each.
d. Relations with those outside the family: Relatives, in-laws, friends, coworkers.
e. Care of the body: Wishes and resolutions you each have for taking better care of your physical health and fitness, and how each can help the other; discuss meals and diet as well.
f. Care of the household: The different domains, how chores are allotted, what needs to be fixed, and long-term goals for improvement.
g. Professional work: Its demands and worries, how each can help the other, what needs to change.

Procedure. Take notes on a computer, tablet, or notepad. Make resolutions as regards each topic as appropriate. Agree on the "minutes" (as it were) at the end and agree to review briefly what was resolved at regular intervals during the coming year, for example, during a monthly date night. Each person should have a copy for consultation and bringing to prayer.

In general, husband and wife need to spend time together roughly analogous to how we believe we need to spend time with God in order to have a good relationship with Him. With God, we believe that each day we should pray; each week (minimally) we should worship; each month (as spiritual authors say) we should go to a "day of recollection" (which is a mini-retreat); and each year we should go on retreat. Similarly for a married couple: They should find some time each day to be together and talk; every week or month they should go on a date; and once a year they should go on retreat. Remember Bl. Alvaro del Portillo's advice: The two bonds between spouse and God go hand-in-hand.

Before leaving this topic of friendship between husband and wife, we need to discuss briefly the sometimes-tricky question of how husband and wife should deal with acquaintances of the opposite sex in professional work, charitable activities, or in social circles (whether in the parish or the community).

In general, people wonder whether a man and a woman can be "mere" friends, especially when they are young or in their prime, without the presence in the relationship of some kind of eroticism. The question presents itself differently for unmarried persons, who are looking to get married, and for married persons, who are looking to be loyal and chaste in heart. As this is not a book on dating or courtship, I will discuss only the latter.

The general rule is that a married person should not continue in any association with a member of the opposite sex where it is not clear, and clear to both, that they are relating as brother and sister. (What it means to relate as brother and sister will be a lot clearer to someone from a large family than to a single child. But it means with a relaxed affection that excludes any hint of sexual association.) Here are some prudent rules that should generally be followed:

a. Approach all one-on-one associations with a member of the opposite sex as if it is "you as standing for the married couple" rather than just you on your own. For example, if you are meeting with a coworker for coffee, then it is as if your spouse is virtually present also at that coffee meeting. In particular, you should find yourself in no way trying to hide, block, or exclude from the meeting the consideration of your married state and family.
b. Run all one-on-one meetings past your spouse and attain consent and approval in advance. Certainly do this for all meetings that do not "have to happen" because of a genuine demand of work or a superior's decision, but ideally do so for all meetings. Sharing a common calendar can help. Your spouse's knowing about a meeting and consenting to it helps him or her "be there" with you in intention. It also gives needed accountability. When you clear the meeting with your spouse, your spouse can get a clear understanding of your intentions and would sense if there were any drift in your affections away from professionalism.
c. Communications with any member of the opposite sex should not become personal except in a general way, and occasionally, expressive of the goodwill that anyone has to anyone ("Congratulations on your son's marriage" or "I hope you've gotten over that bad flu"). If the other person seems like he is trying to steer communications away from work matters toward personal matters, or keeps getting in touch without a clear work-related purpose, this should

set off alarm bells. You need to share these facts with your spouse as soon as possible.

d. Never criticize your spouse to a member of the opposite sex. (For that matter, never criticize your spouse to a member of the same sex, except implicitly when seeking advice about how you yourself can act better.)

e. Never share any confidences with a member of the opposite sex except those that are required by work.[7] It should never be the case that someone binds you to withhold something from your spouse (except in work matters where extreme confidentiality is required). If someone does, then, again, alarm bells should ring, and you need to tell your spouse about it immediately.

f. Never seek consolation with a member of the opposite sex. (Our first source of consolation should always be prayer. Have frequent recourse to the Psalms.)

These are some good guidelines which convey a general approach. Each couple will want to adapt any list like this to the facts and circumstances of their own marriage.

---

7. I am not speaking here about relationships with priests and religious. But even then, prudence of course is necessary. That is why traditionally there are grates in confessionals.

8

Friendship Between Parents and Children

The great blessing upon a married couple of the Old Testament was "May you see your children's children." But have you ever considered why this form of words was used? It is not accidental. The purpose of procreation of any kind is to produce a new member of a species just like the parents. But the parents are not simply mature members of that species: They are *ipso facto* also mature members who have procreated. Therefore, they have not succeeded at procreation until they produce mature members who have procreated.

Another way to put the point is that marriage does not attain its complete goal (relative to this world, anyway) until the children who are the fruit of that marriage have grown up, gotten married themselves, and had their own children.[1] Another way to make the same point would be that in a society in which the purpose of marriage was forgotten—say, marriage was taken to be for company or perpetual dating or convenience and pleasure, not procreation—this Old Testament blessing would have no purchase. No one would really care to see their children's children and, therefore, there would be a marked decline in the "total fertility rate"—just as we see today.

Again, in these last sections our aim is to look at marriage and the family specifically through the lens of friendship. Friends are friends of likes, not unlikes. So, it is only when children have grown up and have had children of their own that they become at last like their parents, as parents. Only at this point can a bond form based, between them and their parents, based on likeness and equality between the children as children and the parents as parents.

Therefore, another way to put the point we just made is that marriage attains its goal relative to the world when a married couple can form a bond of equal friendship with their children. One of the fruits of marriage is friendship with one's children.

Obviously, this would be a long-term goal in a newly married couple, the way they might think that one day it would be appealing as old folks to sit together on rocking chairs on a porch and look back on how they fell in love and started a family. And yet, it should be a much more lively goal for them than that. It is not a goal like, say, saving to buy cemetery plots, because it is a goal that should shape from the start how they raise their children. The "finished product" they should have in mind in all their dealings

---

1. That's why the blessing does not, as you might have supposed, initiate an unstoppable infinite regress, "May you see your children's children's children," and so on.

with their children should be marriageable children who want to have children.[2]

Parents who, in contrast, in everything that they say, do, and favor make it clear to their children that their overriding goal is that the child get into a prestigious university or land a lucrative first job—such parents are doing a tremendous harm to their children, to themselves, and to the Church.

You may wonder: "But isn't the higher goal for parents that their children become saints? And many saints, of course, have foresworn marriage."

The second question is easy to answer: Even if some saints have foresworn marriage, they were eminently marriageable when they foreswore it. Indeed, they gain merit from foreswearing marriage, because they are very well positioned to enjoy the natural and divine goods of marriage. But God's will for them is for something higher.

As for the first question: How could it be the case that marriage is the path for sanctity for a married couple but raising appropriately the children of that marriage is not? Or how is a couple permitted to make a divorce between sanctity and marriage as regards their children—in the absence of any indication of a special calling to the celibate state—if they are not permitted to divorce these things in their own life? Remember too that we are not conceiving of procreation as biological solely for a Christian. Christians bring their children to baptism, and therefore they are procreating, in imitation of Mary and of the Church, children of God and citizens of the kingdom of heaven.

---

2. We must say "marriageble" rather than "married," and "want to have children" rather than "have children," because it is in God's hands whether one finds a spouse and whether a couple is fertile.

I am not saying that being marriageable and wanting to have children is the only goal parents should strive for in their children, but rather that it is a highly important goal, often neglected, of eternal significance, that should condition everything else that they do in raising their children.

Parents also make their children like themselves, and therefore befriendable to them, through educating them. Two types of education are important for fostering friendship between parents and their children: (1) education in what is common to all Catholics and important, and (2) education in what the parents in particular know.

(1) By "education in what is common to all Catholics and important," I mean the teachings of the Church, lives of saints, history of the Church, great Christian literature, and great Christian art and music. These areas are the best foundation for a future friendship. The reason is that children will vary tremendously in other respects. Some will love classical music and others classic rock. Some will love golf, whereas some will see no attraction in the sport but will instead love flying airplanes. These are just examples. The point is that, with a view to friendship, parents should emphasize in education those matters that they can expect all Christians to esteem, because the Church proposes them to the entire human race to be esteemed. Love of classical music cannot be guaranteed in one's Christian children (or anything else: Fill in the blank). But love of Mary can. And because these matters involve the deepest aspirations of the human heart, they are the best suited for a bond of genuine friendship.

By the way, these reflections explain why children who are homeschooled or attend faithful Catholic schools will be on a much better path to forming eventually a good friendship with their parents than children who attend secular schools.

(2) But parents should also educate their children, to the extent that they can, in matters in which they have a particular expertise. The reason is that this makes the children like the parents through the conveyance, as it were, of some "part" of the parents to the children.

Parents often neglect this task because they think they have no time for it, or because they have completely outsourced all education of their children to teachers in schools. (Recall that parents are the primary educators of their children. They cannot escape that responsibility, and therefore accountability for it before the throne of God, because others serve as their agents.) In picking something to convey to your children, look for the more universal and the more immediately practical. For example, suppose a father as a young man worked as a carpenter but then later, for the security and salary, took a desk job at an insurance agency. He might choose to teach his sons carpentry before attempting to explain to them the insurance business (although the latter is certainly valuable), because carpentry has a more universal utility and is more immediately practical. Obviously, it will be time-consuming to teach them carpentry. It really will amount to holding a small job on the side. If he has carpentry projects around the house, bringing in his unskilled sons will slow him down. It would be a long while before they actually contributed more than they "cost." However, he must keep reminding himself that his purpose in teaching his children is the "social bond," not efficiency.

Naturally, it helps for the parents to have this kind of proficiency in the first place. One of the best reasons for a mother to become skilled at particular crafts around the household, say, "artisanal sourdough" baking, is that this is a highly desirable, universal, and practical skill, which she can pass on to her daughters and share with them. Or what good was someone's liberal education in music or literature unless some of it gets shared with one's children? Reading aloud has many benefits, but one of its chief fruits is the forming of a common bond of culture between parents and children. Again, none of this is easy and will require similar self-discipline to that used in a resolution to go on the treadmill for thirty minutes a day without fail.

Education in shared culture is largely a matter of showing something to a child and simply saying, "Look!"—and you look at it and wonder about it together—whether this be the Grand Canyon, a sports championship on television, a classic movie like *North by Northwest*, a poem you once memorized, the design of some machine, or masterpiece paintings in a museum.[3] The key is to spend time doing this. There is no better use of your time than spending it with your children. If you "see" things with your children, you help to demolish the idea that there are two cultures, "adult" things and "kids and family" things. And so, when later your teenage children come to you and ask whether they are permitted to watch this-and-such movie, you can say, "Would I watch it? Would you and I watch it together?" And they understand that you have only one standard.

A shared culture is fostered crucially by conversations over the dinner table as the children get older. Some families leave a newspaper or magazine on the table that the children will peruse over breakfast or at other times.[4] These sources provide starting points

---

3. Teaching children what movies are great and how to watch them is highly important.

4. So few of them remain good. At the time of the writing of this book, *The Wall Street Journal* seems the best. But even this paper contains a great deal of ideological reporting, and its ads and stories currently push an agenda of sexual libertinism.

for dinner-table conversations. The father and mother should start thoughtful conversations deliberately, in a manner appropriate to the older children, for example "Have you followed the debate in the *Journal* as to whether tariffs will cause inflation?" (You might need to explain what a tariff is and define *inflation*. You might even need to state the main argument on each side to get the conversation going.) It will be good for the smaller children to sit quietly and listen as they are told. But also, the parents and older children profit by trying to explain something to the younger children. But if the whole exercise breaks down on any evening because of chaos, it's no big deal; at least you gave it a try.

A difficult transition for many parents, especially fathers, is that from when the children act like a single "pack," who follow the father spontaneously, whatever he suggests, as if he were the pied piper, to when they begin to act with greater individual choice and don't easily consent to something if they are not individually approached and persuaded. Children begin to break away from "pack" behavior when they are between ten and fourteen years old. At this age, parents need to begin distinguishing what "the older children" do from "the rest of the children." It's unreasonable for parents to presume that all of the family members must always do things together without exceptions. Rather, one of the fascinating pleasures of a large family is how so many different combinations are possible of its members in subgroups. Members of a family need to develop the sense of always being part of the family even when they are away from the family. They will acquire this from how the father and mother act, and will follow the lead. Are the father and mother always doing things as one, even if they are doing different work in different places?

To make progress in the interior life, one needs to get used to wasting time—of course not actually wasting time but appearing to waste time relative to work which, on its surface, makes the claim of being "truly serious" and important. The same can be said about developing bonds of friendship with one's children. Do not let special opportunities pass you by—they are too precious!

For the mother especially, she has to be prepared to stay up well beyond when she is exhausted because a teenage child has come down to the kitchen when everyone else has gone to sleep and wants to talk heart-to-heart. (Why is it always the mother, and always in the kitchen, and always when everyone else is going to sleep? There are deep reasons.) Fathers won't as easily be faced with such precious times; rather, they must engineer them. Some dads like to have spaces that say, "Come in here and talk whenever you like." This what the traditional "den" was for. But in that case, the dad must really make it clear that the child truly is welcome to talk by putting down his work or entertainment immediately and giving his full attention when a child comes in. But fathers will find that sons generally like to raise deep topics when they are already doing something challenging side-by-side, like building a deck together or going on a long hike with heavy packs. Road trips or camping trips as a rite of passage, when a son is around fifteen, are excellent ideas. The conversations will have a lasting effect even if they are forgotten. You won't know what you've lost if you allow work to crowd it out.

For a daughter, a father should take her out on dates, treating her as a lady, as he would his wife, almost as if he were courting her. It's not necessary to go overboard in this. (If a dad has four daughters, to take each on a date once a month would bankrupt a family on a modest income.) In truth, a single date at the right time in a daughter's life can teach such things as how to dress up, how a gentleman acts, how to place an order in a fine restaurant, and how to carry on an adult conversation—and the statement it makes from the father about his daughter's dignity is unsurpassable and definitive. For "dates" between sons and moms, the initiative will typically come from the son, and it will not actually take the form of a "date," so much as an occasion where he can take the dad's place somehow in "serving and protecting." For example, the son wakes up early to make the mom breakfast in bed, or cook pancakes for the family, just as dad does.

Because facts and circumstances are so varied, perhaps the best advice one can give in this matter is to seek advice. Parents might form discussion groups with other parents to discuss specifically the question of how to raise children who become your friends as adults. Younger parents who are just starting out should find ways of learning from older parents who have experience, including those who realize they made terrible mistakes and want to help a younger generation avoid the same.

CONCLUSION

In all matters of friendship, which rest upon matters of the heart, we should turn to Our Lady. We invoke her as a special patroness of the family and, in view of her intervention at Cana, a powerful intercessor and friend of all married couples. We can also invoke her as the patroness of friendship under the title "Mother of Fair Love." In this regard, let us follow these words of St. Alphonsus Liguori:

> *He that is a friend loveth at all times, and a brother is proved in distress,* says the Book of Proverbs. We can never know our friends and relatives in the time of prosperity; it is only in the time of adversity that we see them in their true colors. People of the world never abandon a friend as long as he is in prosperity; but should misfortunes overtake him, and more particularly should he be at the point of death, they immediately forsake him. Mary does not act thus with her clients. In their afflictions, and more particularly in the sorrows of death, the greatest that can be endured in this world, this good Lady and Mother not only does not abandon her faithful servants, but as, during our exile, she is our life, so also

> is she, at our last hour, our sweetness, by obtaining for us a calm and happy death.[1]

And let us pray with St. Alphonsus this prayer:

> Ah, my Immaculate Lady! I rejoice with thee on seeing thee enriched with so great purity. I thank, and resolve always to thank, our common Creator for having preserved thee from every stain of sin; and I firmly believe this doctrine, and am prepared and swear even to lay down my life, should this be necessary, in defense of this thy so great and singular privilege of being conceived immaculate.
>
> I would that the whole world knew thee and acknowledged thee as being that beautiful "Dawn" which was always illumined with divine light; as that chosen "Ark" of salvation, free from the common shipwreck of sin; that perfect and immaculate "Dove" which thy divine Spouse declared thee to be: that "enclosed Garden" which was the delight of God; that "sealed Fountain" whose waters were never troubled by an enemy; and finally, as that "white Lily," which thou art, and who, though born in the midst of the thorns of the children of Adam, all of whom are conceived in sin, and the enemies of God, wast alone conceived pure and spotless, and in all things the beloved of thy Creator. Permit me, then, to praise thee also as thy God himself has praised thee: *Thou art all fair, and there is not a spot in thee*,[2] O most pure Dove, all fair, all beautiful, always the friend

---

1. Alphonsus Maria de'Liguori, and Eugene Grimm, *The Glories of Mary*, 4th print rev. ed. (Redemptorist Fathers, 1931), p. 99.

2. "*Tota pulchra es, amica mea, et macula non est in te.*" Song 4:7.

of God. *O how beautiful art thou, my beloved! how beautiful art thou.*[3]

Ah, most sweet, most amiable, immaculate Mary, thou who art so beautiful in the eyes of thy Lord,—ah, disdain not to cast thy compassionate eyes on the wounds of my soul, loathsome as they are. Behold me, pity me, heal me. O beautiful lodestone of hearts, draw also my miserable heart to thyself. O thou, who from the first moment of thy life didst appear pure and beautiful before God, pity me, who not only was born in sin, but have again since baptism stained my soul with crimes. What grace will God ever refuse thee, who chose thee for his daughter, his Mother, and Spouse, and therefore preserved thee from every stain, and in his love preferred thee to all other creatures? I will say, in the words of St. Philip Neri, "Immaculate Virgin, thou hast to save me." Grant that I may always remember thee; and thou, do thou never forget me.

The happy day, when I shall go to behold thy beauty in Paradise, seems a thousand years off; so much do I long to praise and love thee more than I can now do, my Mother, my Queen, my beloved, most beautiful, most sweet, most pure, Immaculate Mary.

Amen.[4]

---

3. "*Quam pulchra es, amica mea, quam pulchra es!*" Song 4:1.

4. Alphonsus Maria de' Liguori, *Glories of Mary*, pp. 316–317.

APPENDIX: HOW TO HAVE A REALLY GREAT NAVIGATOR'S CONFERENCE

Idea: A marriage is like a noble seafaring vessel; it plumbs deep waters and shallow ones alike; it takes adventures, and sometimes sits in dry dock for needed repair; sometimes it goes in the right direction, other times it is woefully off course. Husband and wife are co-navigators of this ship. There are not two ships, but only one. Periodically, the navigators should meet together to talk explicitly about the quality of the ship and the upbringing of the young which are brought to being in its warm and nurturing decks—the goal is to "assess" the current state, to "describe anew the common ideal," and to "chart" the course to that ideal.

HOW OFTEN?

(1) Once a year is the absolute minimum time that can pass before a ship needs to be put into dry dock for repair—thus, this should be done annually, in full form, once a year.

(2) We recommend a monthly "mini" navigator's conference. One nice idea is to pick the day of the month corresponding to the date of your wedding (or the closest available evening).

FORMAT FOR A FULL NAVIGATOR'S CONFERENCE

This takes at least a weekend, like a retreat. Go anywhere private but also restful (that is, don't go on a rock climbing trip). Places that afford opportunities for walking (or light hiking) are ideal. Bring a special notebook, or a laptop computer, or something else that you find useful for recording conversations, inspirations, and conclusions. You can't chart the course without writing anything down. Begin and end conversations with a prayer to the Holy Spirit for guidance, and be sure to fit in Mass and a Rosary each day too.

Friday evening (and the drive to your destination): Spend the first day and/or evening talking about your ideals—use some good material on marriage. Get charged up and excited about what you want to create together with the help of God. Talk too about your ideals for your children. What are you especially attracted to in other families, marriages, and children? Identify your role models (they can be living families that you know or saints, perhaps).

Saturday: Spend the day relaxing. Except for meals, spend as much time as possible in isolated places where you can talk in complete privacy. A hotel room or bed and breakfast room may suffice, but the best conferences can happen while walking in the woods, hiking, or even cross-country skiing together. Fresh air and the beauty of nature are helpful.

Over the course of the day, work through assessments. Keep notes. First, assess your marriage. How are you doing? Is it as great as you dreamed it would be, or does it fall short in some ways? How so? What sorts of things cause ongoing fights/arguments/disputes? (Usually there are some recurring disagreements.) Take turns asking each other which things make you happiest about your marriage and which things disappoint you the most. Ask your spouse openly which are the top three things he or she would want you to work on in the coming year. How is your prayer life—separately and as a couple? Do you pray together? Do you pray for each other? Do you know the deepest spiritual aspirations of your spouse? You can find more good questions and topics for discussion in a good book on marriage or parenting—and you might bring two or three along with you—look for works by Gregory Popcak (marriage), Jim Stenson (parenting), Meg Meeker (parenting), Art and Laraine Bennett (temperament and marriage), Jim and Staci Eldredge (relationships) and other titles that may be available in a solid Catholic bookstore. But look for a recommendation from trusted friends.

Then, after wrestling through the sometimes-painful process of marital assessment and taking good notes, proceed to discussing your children. Spend a lot of time thinking about each child. Consider the four aspects of the proper formation of your children: physical, emotional/psychological, social, and spiritual. Try to assess how each child is doing in each respect, and think about areas that are really strong and areas that might need help. Discuss special issues that might need attention (ongoing bad habits or attitude issues). Also, discuss things that might be on the horizon, and anticipate rules you might need to make (do you have a preteen that might start asking about dating and coed parties soon?). As above, collect two or three books on parenting from a good source and have them handy so that you have material for discussion in case you run out of things to think about.

Sunday: This is the celebration of the Resurrection and going forward. Chart your new course together. Going over your notes, starting with your marriage, make a list of ideas, resolutions, and inspirations that will help you get from the assessment point (where you are at) to the ideals you discussed. Try to keep your list of things manageable—you can't do everything at once. Agree on the things that are priorities and come up with some practical steps you can take. (Note: this is an example of something which is *not* practical: "We will strive to have more time to talk about our day together"—but this is something *practical*: "We will throw away the television that is in our bedroom and spend thirty minutes before bed talking with each other.")

After this, work through each of your children. Come up with some concrete steps you can take to improve their formation: books they should read, courses they might take, time they might spend with one or both of you (dads and daughters, mothers and sons). Perhaps more radical steps are needed—new schools, new weekend activities, or new friends. Perhaps there are simple things—arranging the music lessons you have been putting off. Get some action items for each area of their formation and write up a plan.

Celebrate at the end of your weekend!

FORMAT FOR A NAVIGATOR'S MINI-CONFERENCE

Once a month (or as often as possible), take your notebook to a quiet place and review your plans, inspirations, commitments, and resolutions. Make a note of any progress that has been made. Check off items that have been accomplished. And keep notes that may be relevant for the next *full* conference. A great way to do this monthly conference is to start with prayer before the Blessed Sacrament and follow it up with a dinner out or some other concentrated time together.